Praise

'Brilliant, brilliant book. Excellently crafted, very well structured and superbly written. Loved your simple examples used to explain the complicated strategies.'
 — **Owen O'Malley**, CEO of The Investment Club network, with over 200 member clubs

'This book offers a great combination of simple explanations and a higher level of detail that will satisfy those who require it.'
 — **Acer and Andrew Morgan**, members of four extraordinary investment clubs

'Jeff's book is a fantastic manual for an extraordinary trading system, which takes readers step by step through the principles of safe yet successful trading, and the numbers speak for themselves. I would recommend it to anyone who, like me a few years ago, is looking to enter the world of financial markets in the smartest and safest possible way with a view to securing financial freedom.'
 — **Kasia Muszynska**, NHS Project Manager

'The knowledge embodied in this book has allowed me to restore my planned retirement date after pension changes blew it way off course.'
 — **Michael Smith**, Fire Officer

'Honest, straightforward and easy to understand. This book perfectly captures and explains the trading system.'
— **Paul Elliott**, Police Officer

'I always believed the stock market was for rich people and the best I could aspire to was an ISA – what a game changer trading is!'
— **Pat Chambers**, NHS Hospital Foundation Trust, Charity Lead

THE
EXTRA
ORDINARY
INVESTMENT
CLUB

YOUR PATH
TO FINANCIAL
FREEDOM

JEFF FITZPATRICK

Re^think

First published in Great Britain in 2023
by Rethink Press (www.rethinkpress.com)

© Copyright Jeff Fitzpatrick

While this book could help anyone with any level of wealth, I dedicate it to those I most want to help. So many people needlessly end up at retirement with what, by any measure, are inadequate financial resources to support what they see as just a reasonable lifestyle. They include:

Private and public sector workers, including WASPIs (Women Against State Pension Inequality) who now work longer, pay more into pension funds and get less out, while retiring later.

Self-employed people and small business owners crushed by recessions, pandemics, late-paying customers and a thousand other travails.

Those thrown out of work in middle age when well-paid alternative employment is almost impossible to find. Many are left with long periods between the end of their working life and pension age, with a large income hole to fill.

Young people – as well as the young at heart – looking to finance a lifestyle change. Perhaps they would like to travel, volunteer, work in the arts or whatever, but need to earn a living too.

May they all prosper.

Contents

Disclaimer

In their involvement with the extraordinary investment clubs, neither Jeff Fitzpatrick, The Investment
Club Network (TICN) nor anyone else associated with
this work act as stockbrokers, brokers, dealers, or reg-
istered or unregistered investment advisers.

Stock and option markets are highly speculative arenas
in which many people lose money. No stock, option or
trading strategy is recommended to readers. Stock and
option prices are subject to change, second by second,
and any recommendation would be quickly out of
date. Any stock or options mentioned are for illustra-
tive and educational purposes only. It is recommended
that readers seek advice from a professional licensed
stockbroker and independent financial adviser prior
to implementing any investment programme or

financial plan. We do not recommend the use of the services of any specific broker, dealer, adviser, financial planner or other professional.

No investment based on the contents of this book can have a guaranteed outcome. This book describes what the extraordinary investment clubs have done to date. The author can't guarantee that their future performance will reflect their previous performance or that the clubs won't change how they trade in the future according to their democratic will.

Ultimately, readers are responsible for all decisions they make. The author is not in any way liable for the investment outcomes of readers. All trading and investment activities carry a risk of lossmaking. Losses can exceed amounts invested.

Stock and option prices

Throughout this book, share prices have been used to bring examples of trading techniques to life. To ensure that the examples are not misinterpreted as trading or financial advice, the prices given are not actual prices but are typical for the stock at the time of writing. Stock prices change by the minute and the examples should not be used as actual prices.

Option prices also change constantly and expire on a given date. The prices shown are therefore also typical examples rather than actual prices and should not be treated as such.

Trader profiles

Throughout this book we have used, with permission, a series of trader profiles. These are the true reflections of the motivations and successes of actual members of the extraordinary investment clubs. Their names have been altered for the purpose of privacy. However, if you would like to make contact with any or all of them, your details can be forwarded.

To make contact, email jeff@myinvestmentclub. co.uk. We also facilitate member contact through the unmoderated WhatsApp groups operated by each club. The groups welcome prospective members joining as guests.

Foreword

It is tragic that many people at the age of sixty-five are either dead or dead broke. Given the prevailing economic conditions of our time, the number of people facing hardship at retirement will likely increase.

More than twenty-five years ago, I attended a Tony Robbins 'Wealth Mastery' class at which more than a dozen of the world's richest people who had made their wealth from the stock markets were present. After hearing them speak, I developed the trading system that you will read about in this book. It has grown and developed over the years with the input of Jeff Fitzpatrick.

I have known Jeff and worked with him for over twenty years. He is one of the top traders I know and by far the best person, from the many I have known, at supporting investment clubs. Among thousands of users, no one else has developed processes like his to maximise the performance of my system.

Jeff is not only a great trader and club supporter, his strong values drive him to share the goal of my partner Ana Rodriguez and me to bring wealth to as many people as possible. He always ensures that even the most modest contributors to club trading funds have a bright financial future.

Almost anyone can significantly improve their financial position using the techniques described in this book. However, nothing will change for any reader unless they act upon what they read. It is not our circumstances that are important. We all live in the same environment of economic turmoil caused by a myriad of factors. As Jeff is proving, significant improvement is more than possible, even in the darkest of times. It is too easy, and a waste of time, to blame circumstances. The important thing is how we react to them.

Help is available. You don't have to do this alone. The team behind this book form your support structure and collectively have over eighty years' experience in this arena. You can, starting today, leverage the thousands and thousands of hours that have gone before your involvement to formulate the powerful, profitable strategies outlined in this life-changing book. Follow this proven system and prepare to be surprised by the awesome power and magic of compounding returns.

Ana and I wish you great success in the future, and remember, it is your decision to act by which your destiny is shaped. Congratulations on finding this book.

Owen O'Malley
Founder and CEO of The Investment Club Network

Introduction

Imagine a dice, numbered like any other. It is not loaded, it is perfect. This is a special dice. No matter how it lands, the thrower wins. Some wins are bigger than others, some take longer to deliver, but every throw wins. Replace the word 'dice' with 'stock trading system' and that is what six extraordinary investment clubs have right now.

All 300+ members of the clubs are building wealth. Some invest as little as £100 per month, others invest hundreds of thousands of pounds. All achieve the same percentage return. They aren't getting rich quick, but they will get rich. The programme works to a time horizon of five to ten years.

I recognise that the above is a big, audacious statement but I will demonstrate that it is fair and you will have as many opportunities as you want to speak with any or all the club members to verify its veracity.

We live in difficult times in which many people have taken a major hit to their finances. Recessions and the pandemic have taken their toll. However, the damage is far worse than most people realise. Structural changes in the economy abound. Some sectors, including hospitality, tourism and retail, have seen many redundancies. Many small businesses have folded and employment patterns have altered with the rise of zero-hours contracts and the gig economy.

There are also changes to pension arrangements. We have seen the wholesale replacement of final salary pension schemes with far less beneficial contribution-based plans. Retirement ages and contribution rates have increased while pensions have reduced. Just ask the WASPI campaigners what they think and feel about pension changes. Too many people have an inadequate pension provision and don't believe they can put things right.

Everyone is fed up with low returns on their savings and investments. Let me demonstrate how poor the returns delivered by the finance industry are... Savings rates of 1% per annum are common. A simple rule of thumb calculation demonstrates the issue. Start with the number 72 and divide it by the rate of return you are 'enjoying'. For example, for an interest rate of 1%, divide 72 by 1 to get the answer 72 to find out how long it takes to double the savings pot. Yes, it takes about 72 years to double savings at 1% per annum. That is without tax or inflation being considered.

We are now seeing how devastating the effects of inflation can be. The cost of fuel, food and many other goods and services is rising steeply while incomes are not. Inflation needs to be taken account of in any financial plan. What better way to do it than with an income stream that increases well ahead of it?

Most people are not looking for great wealth. All they want is a secure income that supports what they consider to be a reasonable lifestyle. A holiday or two, presents for children and grandchildren, being able to help them complete their education or to get onto the housing ladder. It is not a lot to ask.

This book represents an opportunity to fight back. For those who need it, a move towards financial security or even financial independence could start here with a giant step on the path to financial education.

You are about to find out about a diverse group of people who decided that enough is enough and are taking matters into our own hands. We – yes, I am one of them – are successful stock market traders making returns that are transforming our finances.

As well as more mature people worried about retirement income, we have younger members supporting lifestyles of travel and avoidance of the 'daily grind'. Often, they want the freedom to pursue other things. They may want to work in the arts, sport or charities while still having a decent income. They may want to overcome lower income earning potential caused by a medical condition of their own or a family member.

There are also members who already have levels of wealth that many would be happy with. Everyone is welcome. All we ask is that those who join us have decent values and are like-minded people.

After a career in the corporate world, I decided to use my experience to help others. I believe the best way to do this is to enable people to take charge of their own destinies. With that in mind, I set up a business that helped people to get into self-employment. My team and I helped more than 5,000 people to do so with a high level of success.

My next attempt to help was to join the North East Ambulance Service NHS Trust as deputy chair. I like to think that some good was done, particularly as I also chaired the finance committee. I served for six years, but found this to be an arms-length way of helping others.

In 2020 I decided to teach others to do what I do best: make money! I had successfully traded the stock market and owned good businesses for the best part of twenty years. I knew I could give people control of their financial futures. The extraordinary investment club format is the vehicle I chose to achieve it.

My own trading journey started more than twenty years ago. Along the way I have paid off my mortgage, built a good pension, enjoyed a lovely lifestyle and supported my family.

Recently, my ambitions have grown exponentially. I now want to bring financial control and security to a million people. The extraordinary investment clubs are eliminating barriers and bringing the financial opportunities of the few to the many. To date, the clubs have grown purely by word of mouth and recommendation through existing members. This book is a step along the road to realising the vision through publicity. It also aims to grow the numbers reached by bringing what we do to people, even if they choose not to be club members.

With the help of some experienced and talented traders, the clubs have grown to around 300 members from nine countries and trade funds of £5 million.

The first investment club began trading in January 2020. Eight members started contributing £100 per month. By September 2021, it had around £24,000 available to invest. The club has a doubling rate of fourteen months, which is about the average of all the clubs. There is no reason why individuals can't repeat this performance. There is little doubt though that many people prefer, and benefit from, communal investment and trading.

It is fair to say that not a single club member had any prior knowledge of stock market trading when they began and some of them still don't! Some members are keen to learn, some maintain a watching brief and others are completely passive.

We expect the doubling rate to come down to twelve months as we move forward. £100 per month gives an average of £600 per year to invest. Five years of doubling this will result in a nest egg of £37,500. That's a return of 525%. If they can keep going for ten years, resisting the temptation to spend the profits, they will get to a value of £1,227,600. That's over 10,000%. Such is the power of compounding returns, but more on that later.

As noble as I think my ambition is, it has not been an easy choice. Sometimes, I believe it would have been easier to just make money and give it away. In the early days I constantly heard cries of 'impossible', 'can't be true' and even 'scam'! Today, I don't have to ask anyone to have faith in what I say. The members spread the word and vouch for the performance.

Everyone is welcome to join one or more of our club WhatsApp groups and to ask any of the members anything that they wish. We don't moderate the chat, apart from keeping the discussion on-topic. Similarly, subject to the agreement of its members, anyone can join the monthly Zoom meetings of any club. There is no cost or obligation.

People say the stock market is scary and risky. It is, if it is not understood. With over 3,000 trades completed, we have not had a single losing one in any club – so not so scary after all! Every meeting is video recorded to keep a full record of decisions and actions taken. This book will walk you through exactly how the members do so well and how you could too.

PART ONE
THE FIELD OF PLAY

There are lots of ways to make lots of money. Some require a lot of money to start off with, some have a high risk of failure and others take many years to bear fruit. Most successful routes to wealth do not involve directly exchanging time for money, unless you are exchanging someone else's time for money.

Some entrepreneurs have made huge sums – occasionally quickly. I am all in favour of setting up businesses; however, the failure rate is brutal. According to the business insurance provider Embroker's website, 90% of start-up businesses fail.[1]

The alternative, for most people, is to take a share in some of the largest and best-performing businesses on the planet. I have the extraordinarily successful CEOs of organisations such as Microsoft, Apple, Starbucks

---

1   Embroker Business Insurance, '106 must-know startup statistics for 2022', www.embroker.com/blog/startup-statistics, accessed 12 September 2022.

and Boston Scientific working their socks off for me. The way to achieve that is through the stock market.

There are well over 30,000 companies on the stock markets of the world that can be invested in and traded publicly. Which are the strongest? Which have share prices that offer good value? In Part One, I will show you how the extraordinary investment clubs identify the stocks they trade.

Of course, no one has a fail-safe way of identifying stocks that are set to rise or fall. Powerful computers, investment fund managers with years of experience and some of the brightest graduates working for them still get things wrong. Few, if any, consistently get things right. At the other end of the spectrum there are home-based traders and traditional investment club members. They tend to use the news media as their source of knowledge to underpin trading and investment decisions. A few of these traders do moderately well – most don't. As far as the stock market is concerned, most of the news in the public domain has already been taken account of in pricing stocks.

The extraordinary investment clubs are in the middle of the price forecasting spectrum. They use professional research and fundamental and technical analysis and get things right in most cases. In Part One, you will see exactly how they do this. However, just as importantly, the clubs don't bank on getting their forecasts of stock price movements right. They use a forgiving, profitable trading methodology that sits alongside their forecasts, but more of that in Part Two.

ONE

Choosing A Stock Market

Among people who trade stock markets there is an understandable preference to trade those that are based where they live. In the UK, I am constantly asked about UK stocks, which I know little about. The decision on which market to trade warrants greater consideration than being an accident of birth.

We now live in a globalised world and have an almost unlimited choice of markets to trade. This has been facilitated by technology. That same technology, together with enabling legal changes, has made it possible for just about anyone to be able to trade most of the world's stock markets. Given that possibility, why would anyone not select the best markets to trade or invest in?

The extraordinary investment clubs have chosen to trade what they see as the world's premier stock markets. Their choice was not based on these markets being 'premier league'. Instead, factors such as available research, the types of trades that are allowed and costs were considered. By the end of this chapter, you should understand their decision and hopefully see good sense in it.

What stock markets?

Think of the world's stock markets as being in a league table. The United States-based New York Stock Exchange (NYSE) and NASDAQ represent the Premier League. Most of the top companies in the world have shares traded on these exchanges. On them you will find non-US-based companies listed, such as BP and Phillips. You will also find many other familiar names, such as Apple, Ford, Starbucks and Disney.

These are also the biggest stock markets in the world. Size is important when it comes to stock markets. A larger market has more liquidity, which means more trades are taking place and it is easier for them to match buyers and sellers. Stocks can only be bought or sold if there is a market for them – that is if someone is prepared to buy what is being sold and to sell what is being bought.

Companies listed on the NYSE and NASDAQ stock markets tend to have a lot more information about them in the public domain. This is of massive importance as it is this information that we use to assess and rank stocks.

There is another advantage available to those who trade stocks on these markets. This one almost trumps all others. The extraordinary investment clubs could not use their trading techniques without it. It relates to the trading of stock options. That is the ability to sell promises to *buy* stocks at given prices by set dates and to sell promises to *sell* stocks at given prices by set dates.

Although this ability is also available in respect of other stock markets, including the London Stock Exchange and European markets, there are vital differences that give unique advantages in the way that option trading operates in the US.

Finally, buying and selling stocks usually involves a cost. Brokers, market makers and others earn their money through spreads and commissions. Spreads are just the (usually) small differences between the prices that stocks are bought and sold at. Commissions and spreads costs tend to be lower in the US compared to other markets.

Learning from history and compound returns

The advantages of using the main US markets to trade are considerable. However, they mean nothing unless we can see and measure success. Success, in this instance, is relative; it is about measuring club performance against the overall performance of the market.

Measuring relative success involves looking back over time at performance against a yardstick. The extraordinary investment clubs see the Standard and Poors 500 (S&P 500) as the best available yardstick. The S&P 500 is an index of the value of stocks made up of 500 of what most people consider to be large companies across all industrial sectors. Size, in this case, is measured by market capitalisation. This is calculated for each individual company by multiplying the number of shares issued to the market by the current price of those shares. Size is not the only qualification for inclusion in the S&P 500, but it is by far the most important.

There are other yardsticks such as the Dow Jones Top 30 and the NASDAQ. The former measures the market capitalisation of only the top thirty companies. The latter measures stocks that are listed only on the NASDAQ stock market. Most of the world's top investors and traders see thirty as being too small a sample and the NASDAQ as being overly biased towards technology companies.

It is possible to buy and sell shares in a fund that owns all the companies that form the S&P 500. Many commentators recommend doing exactly that. After all, the S&P 500 is diverse and changes as some companies get large enough to be included and others shrink to drop out. Typically, investing in the collective S&P 500 returns around 12% per annum. Investing in it is also a relatively low-cost affair as it doesn't incorporate expensive fund managers and generally involves fewer trades and therefore lower costs than, for example, managed funds.

Logic tells us that size isn't everything and that some companies in the S&P 500 must perform better and represent better value than others. The clubs use a range of measures to determine whether a company is fundamentally sound and if its stock represents value for money. That said, fund managers do the same and, as noted above, few of them – if any – are consistently successful. It is possible to be correct more often than not, as legendary investors Warren Buffett and his partner Charlie Munger have shown (though not all of their selections have worked out well).

The trading system used by the clubs owes a lot to Buffett and Munger and performs relatively well in identifying stocks. The system doesn't get it right all the time, but the stocks it identifies collectively and consistently outperform the S&P 500 for average growth in value.

You will learn, as you progress through this book, that the clubs don't only rely on picking stocks that go on to grow by the largest percentages. Success also comes from how the clubs trade. Essentially, they take advantage of being relatively small players and can use types of trade that the professionals can't. For example, according to *Investor's Business Daily*, Warren Buffett's company, Berkshire Hathaway, owns about 10% of the Coca-Cola company.[2] If he decided to buy more shares, he would pay the current price, which at the time of writing is $62.87 per share. If a club chose to trade Coca-Cola shares (and by the way, they don't) then they could, at current prices, offer to buy them for $62.50 each in the future and be paid a premium of $3.60 – probably a little more with some negotiation – for making that promise. Their effective price would be $62.50 − $3.60 = $58.90. That represents a discount of $3.97, or over 6%, on the current price. Presumably, Warren Buffett would, like the clubs, buy the shares expecting them to rise in price. If the price stayed above $62.50 no one would want to sell the shares to the clubs at that price. They would just keep the $3.60. Clubs can undertake such trades because they are dealing with small numbers of shares. The trade could not take place with 10% of them because the brokers would not be able to find owners of 10% of Coca-Cola shares who were prepared to sell at $62.50, having paid out a premium of $3.60 for the privilege.

Similarly, if the clubs did end up owning the shares, they could sell the right to someone to buy them from the club at a price and by a set date that the members were happy with. The clubs would be paid for selling the right to have shares taken from them. Usually, the

---

2 *Investor's Business Daily*, 'Warren Buffett stocks: what's inside Berkshire Hathaway's portfolio?', www.investors.com/research/warren-buffett-stocks, accessed 12 October 2021.

premium they receive is around 5–10% of the selling price. Again, this wouldn't work if anyone was trying to sell 10% of the Coca-Cola company.

I should make it clear that I have no idea whether Warren Buffett is interested in buying more Coca-Cola shares and that the clubs currently are not. I have used the above as an illustration only, albeit using current prices and premium levels.

Compound growth

The S&P 500 index has been measuring the stock market in its current form since March 1957. The value changes constantly, every fifteen seconds during the trading day, to reflect changing share prices.

A graph (or as traders refer to it, a chart) of the S&P 500 index shows exponential growth. The growth is frequently interrupted by world events such as wars, recession, the pandemic, etc. To date it has overcome everything thrown at it and reverted to what looks like a pattern of eternal growth. Some researchers have extended the chart back in time to cover the Great Depression of 1929 and other major events such as the First World War. They have invariably found that the growth pattern has re-emerged whatever the event.

The underlying growth pattern is one of compounding growth in the value of the top 500 companies. In general, it has taken an average of around six to seven years to double in value. The nature of compound growth (also known as exponential growth) is such that the doubling rate reduces as time progresses.

As I hinted at earlier, being in the S&P 500 does not mean that a company meets every condition required for the clubs to classify it as being a fundamentally sound business that they would like to trade the shares of. Many S&P 500 companies don't get onto the club watchlists because they fall short of the clubs' standard needed for fundamentally sound business status.

The clubs also look for stocks that represent great value for money. They use several factors to determine which stocks offer good value. For example, one factor is the price to earnings ratio (or P/E ratio). This ratio measures the price of shares compared to their earnings, also known as profits!

In some cases, the P/E ratio is high. At the time of writing, the ratio for eBay was well over 200, while that of US Steel was just 1.48. That means a share in eBay is currently set to take over 200 years to pay for itself through profits, while shares in US Steel generate enough profit to cover their share price in less than eighteen months. Historically, prices of stocks with high P/E ratios tend to fall faster and further than those with low P/E ratios when the stock market has pullbacks and bear markets.

We will put the S&P 500 to one side for now. For the moment, we will concentrate on how the clubs identify fundamentally sound stocks that offer great value, whether they are part of the S&P 500 index or not.

TRADER PROFILE

Paul Middleton is a fire officer. The Fire Service Pension Fund was altered a few years ago, not in a good way. The changes required him to pay more money in and to work to an older age, which would result in him getting a lower pension.

Paul joined an extraordinary investment club in 2020, putting £100 per month into the trading pot. Had he been trading by himself, at that rate it would have taken him many years to achieve a personal trading pot value of $25,000. That is the value needed to access the type of trade that the clubs use so successfully. Had he just traded a personal account, he may or may not have had the time or inclination to learn how to trade well. He would probably not even have come across the trading methods used by his club. By trading as part of a club, he, together with the other members, was able to benefit from reaching the $25,000 threshold after about nine months. He is now well over 100% up in account value and hasn't suffered a single loss.

Paul's daughter, a trainee nurse, has now joined the club. Her options on retirement and life choices will be vastly better than those of her father because of the additional years of trading ahead of her.

Summary

In this first chapter, we looked at why the NYSE and the NASDAQ are the best stock markets in the world for the extraordinary investment clubs to trade. Their size, liquidity, volatility, the lower cost of trading and the availability of good, detailed information about the companies being traded put these stock markets firmly in first position by themselves. However, the fact that the uniquely US style of option trading is available on them makes these markets win hands-down.

We also covered an example of how small traders can frequently trade more successfully than large institutions, with the Coca-Cola trade showing how this can work in practice.

The groundwork has been set for determining how traders, including the extraordinary investment clubs, can measure their progress using the frequently used comparator of the S&P 500.

It was demonstrated that generation of compound returns is key to the success of the extraordinary investment clubs. It was noted that the nature of compounding growth is such that it starts relatively slowly but has an increasingly fast doubling rate. Eventually, the growth curve becomes almost vertical.

In Chapter 2 we will begin to focus in on identifying individual stocks within the NYSE and NASDAQ markets that have the potential to generate significant gains for the clubs.

TWO
Fundamental Analysis

In this chapter we are going to stand on the shoulders of giants. There are many 'giants' in the world of stock trading and investment. I am referring here to the all-time greats of investing like Warren Buffett and Sir John Templeton, who belong to a class of investors known as 'value investors'. They concentrate on understanding the fundamental economics of businesses such as profitability, indebtedness, growth rates and similar. This information is used to determine the value for money that stocks offer and to find undervalued companies.

The extraordinary investment clubs have taken lessons from many value investors. The clubs have found sources of data that allow them to benefit from the same techniques used by the 'giants'. The analysis undertaken by the clubs can't be, and isn't, as deep or as detailed as the analysis that the big investors use. However, the record of clubs' successes is extremely good and, at least in part, reflects the quality of the analysis they carry out.

Elements of technical analysis and forgiving trading techniques are also part of the mix; both are examined later in this book. However, it all starts with the identification of fundamentally sound businesses with stocks at prices that offer exceptionally good value. At the end of this chapter, you will know exactly how the clubs identify companies that have great fundamentals and offer great value.

Value Line Inc.

There are around 12,000 stocks listed on the combined NYSE and NASDAQ stock exchanges. Therefore, some help is needed to filter them down to a manageable number. A quick, easy way of finding the required information about the companies is also needed. The hard way is to obtain the annual reports of all the companies and then to follow any news and updates available.

You will be pleased to hear that there is a quick and easy way to get the information. The clubs use the reports and updates produced by a research company called Value Line Inc. The company was established after the Great Depression and stock market crash of 1929. Its sole purpose is to provide honest, reliable information on businesses for the use of investors. They are wholly independent.

Value Line don't provide detailed reports on every company that is listed on the NYSE or NASDAQ. The company only produces full reports on around 1,700 businesses that they have identified as good, sound enterprises. This helps the clubs by eliminating about 85% of the candidate stocks.

In addition, Value Line subscribers have a bespoke filtering tool. This generates lists based on user-defined parameters. The clubs use the main factors set out below as filters. They constantly rerun the filters to keep their long list of candidates up to date. The long list usually has around 200 stocks on it. The parameters are set tightly, and only around half a dozen new stocks get added to the watchlist each year.

Value Line reports also form an integral element of the trading system by providing stock price forecasts. These are based on the medium term being twelve to eighteen months, and the long term being three to five years. According to Value Line, their forecast has been 85%+ correct over the last ninety years or so. Their forecasts are conservative and provide a range that the price is expected to fall within, rather than a single price point.

The clubs are in good company. Warren Buffett and Charlie Munger have said on record that they use Value Line data and that no one should even think about trading without it.[3] The extraordinary investment clubs use the collective buying power of TICN to give all members direct subscriber access to the Value Line reports.

Fundamentally sound companies

While being 'fundamentally sound' seems great, traders need to understand what is meant by the term. The clubs use seven main factors, as detailed below, to produce what they call a 'quality score' to represent fundamental soundness. The unique scoring system gives a maximum of fifty-two points for quality. Ideally, candidates should achieve a score of forty points or more. However, the clubs will accept a score of between thirty and thirty-nine points, particularly if the stock also represents great value.

Q1 Industry rank

The first of the quality factors is industry rank. Good candidate stocks are expected to be in industrial sectors that have a high potential for growth relative to other sectors. Ideally, the company should be in the

---

3   YouTube, 'Warren Buffett & Charlie Munger on the value of historical data', https://youtu.be/I0fCyJtlcGs, accessed 12 October 2022.

top 25% of all industries judged as having the highest potential for growth.

If, for example, we were assessing Microsoft, we would find that it sits within the software industry, which is currently ranked third out of ninety-four industrial sectors for growth potential. The coffee shop chain Starbucks is in the restaurant industry, which is currently ranked fifty-fifth for growth potential. Foot Locker, the sports footwear retailer, is in a subdivision of the retail industry called 'soft lines', which is currently ranked at a lowly eightieth for growth potential.

The clubs wouldn't write a stock off just because it isn't in the top 25%. However, they would penalise its score for being in the second quartile and penalise it even more for being in the third quartile. Being in the bottom 25% is highly likely to make the clubs pass on a stock.

Q2 Timeliness

Stock prices rise and fall at different rates. Some stock prices are volatile and move quickly while others move more slowly; for example, large companies tend to have stock prices that move up or down slowly. Kraft Heinz, the food processor, is an example of a large company with a slow-moving stock price, while Hawaiian Airlines has a fast-moving stock price. Even when companies have a similar performance, the movement in their share prices can vary considerably. The clubs look for stocks with good performance, with stock prices that are responsive to that performance. Value Line categorise timeliness into five levels. Kraft Heinz is currently in the fourth-lowest category and Hawaiian Airlines is in the second level.

The timeliness measure is an assessment of the probable price performance of a stock relative to the approximately 1,700 other stocks reported on in detail by Value Line. This perfectly matches the objective of identifying stocks with prices that are expected to be the fastest rising among fundamentally sound companies.

Q3 Safety

The clubs want to know what level of 'safety' is forecast for their candidates for the coming twelve months. For example, a volatile stock may be more likely to fall than a less volatile stock. The Value Line Safety score measures the total risk of a stock price falling, relative to the other stocks that they monitor closely.

Again, Value Line use five levels of safety. The clubs prefer stocks that are in the highest of these and give fewer points to stocks in successively lower divisions. Starbucks is currently rated as being in the highest level for safety, while US retailer Bed Bath & Beyond is, like many retailers, in turbulent times and in the lowest division of the safety score.

Q4 Debt

Companies that are carrying a relatively high level of debt are not favoured by the clubs. This is not a matter of the value of the debt, rather it is the value of debt compared to market capitalisation (number of shares multiplied by share price).

Indebtedness is calculated as a percentage of market capitalisation, using figures available from the Value Line report. The percentage has been used to provide a debt score. Companies carrying debt that is less than 10% of their capitalisation score the most points. A level of indebtedness of more than 50% is a red flag. In that case, the clubs will normally pass on the stock. However, exceptions are made as some companies work with high debt and consistently post good profits.

Q5 Beta

This factor reflects the volatility of each stock relative to the volatility of the whole stock market. The clubs don't want to end up with a stock that falls by, say, 10% when the market falls by 1%. They say that a rising tide lifts all boats, but the opposite is also true!

To calculate beta scores, Value Line take the volatility of the whole market as being equal to 1.0. Individual stock volatility is then expressed in relation to this. For example, the retailer Bed Bath & Beyond has a beta of

1.45 at present. That is a high beta score, almost high enough to discount the stock from consideration by itself. Starbucks has a beta of 1.05 which puts it in the top level of four divisions that the clubs use.

It is also possible for stocks to have a beta of less than 1.0 and be classed as favourable. However, a low beta score could indicate low volatility, which would result in lower premiums.

Q6 Growth trends

The next factor is growth. This is a reference to the growth rate of both sales revenue and profits, which is referred to as earnings.

It is easier for a small company to increase its sales by a high percentage than it is for a large one. Therefore, different scales are used for small, medium and large companies. By small, the clubs mean companies having revenues of $400 million or less. By large, they mean companies having revenues of $4,000 million or more.

The extraordinary investment clubs are interested in both a five-year history of growth and a five-year projection of growth into the future. Depending on the size of the company, they want to see growth in revenues over the last five years of between 10% and 15% per annum. They also look at the pattern of that growth. Uninterrupted years of growth are favoured over intermittent growth. For earnings, they look for at least 7% annual growth over the last five years and don't want to see any two of the five years with no growth.

Q7 Management

The final quality assessment is of the competence of the management of the business. This is more subjective but is greatly helped by the commentary provided by Value Line. As well as making a general assessment from the commentary, answers to four specific questions are sought:

1. Are profits increasing?
2. Is the management team solid and are they anticipating future trends?
3. How have the management team handled past challenges?
4. Are the management team operating smoothly without any pending lawsuits?

Using the above, a score of between 1 and 4 is given.

Not all factors are equal

All the above factors are key to the assessment of fundamental soundness. Some are more important than others and the factors are weighted according to their importance. Industry ranking and beta get the lowest weighting. Timeliness, safety, debt and management team performance share the middle ranking, and growth trends get the highest weighting.

Don't worry!

Digging out and scoring the above factors from Value Line is much easier than the alternative ways of finding the information. However, even with all the information on a single web page, it can be daunting to find and score the factors. It is made even easier for members of the extraordinary investment clubs. All the scoring is done for members, and the calculations are updated regularly.

Having the scores is not quite enough! Before making any trading decisions, the clubs check out the latest Value Line report on the company involved. It only takes a few minutes but considerably enhances club performance.

Being classed as a fundamentally sound company is not a good enough reason to trade or invest in it. The clubs also need to assess whether the price of the stock represents good value and to see the price forecast for the future.

Stocks that are great value for money

Like the term 'fundamentally sound', 'great value for money' also needs to be defined and measured. Five parameters are used in the assessment of good value.

Good value, to the extraordinary investment clubs, is a measure of stock price compared to the value of the underlying company. When buying – or promising to buy – a stock, the transaction involves buying a small share of an actual business. That business has assets and produces profits. It may or may not pay part of its profits as dividends and it will, hopefully, have a level of stock price appreciation.

Some investors concentrate on the share price in relation to the book value of the business, others on the P/E ratio. The clubs include both, but go further. Here are the factors they use.

P1 Dividends

You may be surprised to learn that the clubs don't like businesses that pay out a lot of their profits as dividends to shareholders. They would prefer them to reinvest most of their profits to help grow their businesses.

The measure used is simple. Did the company pay out more than half of its profit as dividends in the last year? If it didn't, great – it gets the top score. If it did, the score is low.

P2 Estimated price appreciation

The Value Line five-year forecast percentage growth of the stock price is used for this factor. The ideal is a growth rate of over 15% per year. The Value Line forecast gives a range, and the measure used by the clubs is against the high point of the range.

Again, this is simple. If the forecast is for 15% per annum or more, the stock gets the highest score. If not, it gets the lowest score.

P3 Sales versus earnings

The concern here is with the growth rate of both sales revenue and earnings. It looks at the last five years of growth and projected growth for the next five years.

Ideally, earnings should be growing faster than revenues. If that is the case for both the past and the future, the highest score is given. If it is true for neither the past nor the future, the lowest score is given. A middle score is given if only the past or the future, but not both, pass this test.

P4 Price to earnings ratio

Rather than simply considering the current P/E ratio, this factor looks at the ratio in terms of how it stands compared to where it has been over the last five years. A low P/E ratio is preferred to a higher one.

The top score is reserved for instances where the current P/E ratio is below the average P/E ratio of the previous five years. A middle score is allocated if the current P/E ratio is higher than the average, but less than double. If the current P/E ratio is more than double the average of the previous five years, the lowest score is given.

P5 Risk-to-reward ratio

Stock prices don't stand still. They are always moving, and they tend to appear to move between virtual parallel lines, like boundaries, revisiting price points on a regular basis. The highest and lowest price points over previous years are important.

This factor looks at the average highest price and the average lowest price over the last five years. Ideally, the prices in the lowest quartile attract the highest score. Stocks with prices close to the top of their range at the point of entry score low. Such stocks potentially have less scope to increase and further to fall. The risk potential is high, while the reward potential is low.

Weighting

The weighting factor, used to calculate good value, is less complicated than that used for quality, as each of the above parameters is considered extremely important. The only parameter deemed less important is that covering how much of earnings are paid out as dividends. To take this into account we multiply the scores for the other factors by three.

The watchlist

To date, going back more than twenty years, the scoring system has identified only 118 stocks that have scored forty or more points for both quality and value at the same time. Some of these have disappeared due to mergers and acquisitions; others have not been able to maintain their high score. The barrier is set very high.

Sometimes, stocks are traded that are below the threshold if the parameters that pull the score down are known and understood. After carefully reading the full Value Line report, a considered view may be taken on stocks that don't fall too far below the line.

The type of analysis of stocks that we have just walked through is called 'fundamental analysis'. It has narrowed the candidate list down first from around 12,000 to 1,700, and then to around 200 stocks. Many traders use such fundamental analysis alone to select the stocks they trade.

Analysing 1,700 stocks using the above methodology would be a huge amount of work and a never-ending task. Filtering stocks using the tools provided by Value Line can greatly reduce the burden. In addition, members of the extraordinary investment clubs share the task, thus making it manageable.

At present, the clubs have around 200 stocks of sufficient quality and value to merit inclusion in their long list of candidate stocks to consider. This is still far too many. To get to a shortlist, a different type of analysis called 'technical analysis' is used. This concentrates on timing, the characteristics of how each stock moves and a range of mathematical indicators to build a shortlist of good-to-go stocks to trade.

Many traders use only technical analysis. The extraordinary investment clubs use both fundamental and technical analyses to reach their shortlist, then they go a step further and look at the profitability of each potential trade. The product is a list of around a dozen trades, and even they are ranked in terms of their potential profit outcomes.

More of that later – for now we need to concentrate on using technical analysis to bring our candidate list down from around 200 to around 75 stocks to trade. All the stocks in the watchlist have options traded on them. Trading options is a critical part of what the clubs do. You will see how they are used in Part Two.

TRADER PROFILE

Emma and Roger are a young couple. They have decided that there is more to life than working from nine to five at the mercy of someone else. Instead, they are getting ready to travel the world and go for an adventure.

Their investment club, and what it is teaching them about how to trade, is their passport to freedom. Barely eighteen months after getting involved, they are now making firm travel plans. The couple, understandably at their current stage in life, did not have a fortune to invest, and thankfully didn't need too much to get them to where they want to be.

Emma is also a member of the extraordinary investment club's future trader's programme. This provides intensive training and support and is working to make all thirty of its members millionaires. Starting with £6,000 each, the members are working to double their money ten times over. The first doubling occurred within the programme's first six months.

Emma and Roger are about to demonstrate that making significant money from the stock market need not take up too much time and that it can be done from just about anywhere on the planet where there is internet connection. Note, though, the US stock markets open at 9.30am and close at 4.30pm New York time, irrespective of where you happen to be!

Summary

The extraordinary investment clubs won't look twice at a stock unless they consider it to be fundamentally sound and great value. The clubs have taken notice of how some of the world's most successful investors and traders have categorised stocks in terms of these two requirements. They use a set of parameters for each that produces a score and then use a minimum score to filter out those that don't match their requirements.

This filtering process goes all the way back to the work of Benjamin Graham in his book *The Intelligent Investor*.[4] The clubs consider Graham to be the father of fundamental analysis and they are in good company. Warren Buffett, according to Wikipedia, chose his university because Graham taught there[5] and credits much of his success to what he learned from Graham and subsequently built upon.

While fundamental analysis isn't the club's only source of success, it is a major component of it. Gone are the days when an investment club was typified by a couple of (usually old) men in the back room of a pub, picking stocks based on media reporting. They can now identify the best businesses in the best markets in the world. The next stage of how they operate

---

4   B Graham, *The Intelligent Investor* (HarperBus, 2003).
5   Wikipedia, 'Warren Buffett', https://en.wikipedia.org/wiki/Warren_Buffett, accessed 12 October 2022.

takes those companies and determines if they are ready to be traded as well as the entry and the exit points of those trades. For this, they use technical analysis.

THREE
Technical Analysis

You have seen the generation of a 'watchlist' of stocks that the extraordinary investment clubs consider to be fundamentally sound, representing great value at current prices. Next, the clubs go on to identify the stocks that look ready to be traded in terms of timing. Even great stocks that offer excellent value may be at a short-term price high and therefore not be at the point of offering maximum good value. The clubs use technical analysis to find the best entry and exit points. Essentially, that means using price charts, indicators, earnings and news announcements to develop forecasts of price movements for individual stocks.

This is not as complicated as it sounds. Once traders begin to look at stock price charts, they begin to 'get their eye in'. Within a short time, they can interpret them quickly. Just about anyone can read dozens of charts within a quarter of an hour or so. To get to that point requires understanding what to look for, practice and having the right tools in place.

Technical analysis tools

Stock charts are generally provided free when an online trading account is opened. They are just graphs of changes in individual stock prices over time. The clubs mainly use charts that track prices on a daily and weekly basis. However, they are also available for other time periods such as minutes, hours, months and even years.

Like most traders, club traders use a form of stock chart made up of what are known as 'candlesticks'. Each individual candlestick represents a period, which could be a minute, hour, day, month or even a year. The format is the same in all cases. Generally, charts will have two colours of candlestick. Often green is used for periods with a rising price and red for periods with a falling price, but any two colours will suffice. In this book, we are using light grey for candlesticks depicting upward price changes and black for downward price changes. This is how candlesticks work:

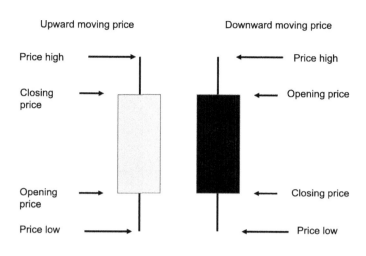

A simple candlestick

Each candlestick gives a wealth of information. They tell us the direction of the price movement in the period they cover, the opening price, how high and low the price moved during the period and the closing price.

When candlesticks from successive periods of time are shown together, they provide information pertaining to longer periods and price movement trends (see below).

There are many trading platforms available and we haven't assessed them all. All the extraordinary investment clubs use a platform called Alpha Plan, provided by a company called Planner Securities.[6] Alpha Plan may not be suitable for all trading. For

---

6   Planner Securities, www.plannersecurities.com, accessed 12 October 2022.

example, it may not be acceptable to UK-based private pension trustees. Club members who trade their own pension accounts have had to find alternative platforms.

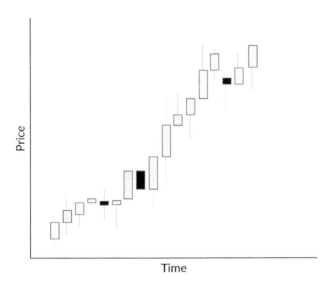

Successive candlesticks

Stock prices tend to visit and revisit the same price points repeatedly. Often, it's as though they are running between invisible tramlines. A price point at which the price trend has turned from up to down may have also been a point at which the trend previously turned from down to up. The line joining the higher points is called 'resistance' and the one joining the lower points is called 'support'.

Some of these points of support and resistance are stronger than others. The stronger ones are those

visited more frequently, which lead to more significant moves after the price has turned.

Traders normally enter trades at strong support price
points, which are probably long-term price lows. That
could mean that the price is lower than it has been for
many months or even years.

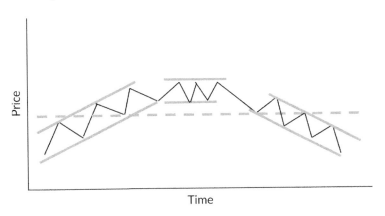

*Stock prices tend to run between invisible 'tramlines': 'support'
is the lower line, while the upper line is 'resistance'. The
dashed line shows how prices tend to use the same points
as support or resistance over time.*

After more than twenty years of trading, it still
astounds me that stock prices frequently move up
and down in sets of three waves or rolls. Often, within
each upward or downward roll, there are three mini
rolls. Therefore, when a stock price is getting to the
top or bottom of a third roll, it may be time to consider action. That could be buying or selling stock, or
options to buy or sell the stock.

These rolls appear irrespective of how short or long the timescale of the chart is. The illustrations above could equally be based on a day, a week, a month or a year. Of course, there are exceptions when the number of rolls is greater or fewer than three. The clubs use indicators to help form a view on whether a stock price has finished a downward or upward trend and is about to start a rising or falling trend.

Indicators

Indicators are statistical measures that overlay stock price charts. There are dozens of different indicators and traders tend to have their favourites. All the extraordinary investment clubs favour and normally use just three of them.

Don't get too hung up on how indicators are calculated; what matters is how they are useful. It's like not needing to know how to write a computer programme to use it for the purpose for which it was written.

Moving averages

The clubs overlay their stock price charts with two moving averages: one of ten days and one of twenty days of average daily prices. These are exponential moving averages, but again, don't worry about the ins and outs of that at this stage; just select the exponential moving average option if you are setting up charts. Also, make sure the two moving average lines are in different colours so chart users can tell which is which!

When the price trend is upward, the ten-day moving average tends to be at a higher level than the twenty-day moving average. Similarly, when the trend is down, the twenty-day moving average tends to be at a higher level than the ten-day moving average.

Instances of the two moving averages crossing over indicate a change of direction in the trend. The ten-day moving average price tends to cut across and run above the twenty-day moving average line when the price is trending upwards. Similarly, when the twenty-day moving average line crosses and runs below the ten-day average line, a downward trend is in progress.

MACD

The moving average convergence and divergence (MACD) is a statistical measure of the moving together and pulling apart of moving averages. This is represented in the form of a histogram with its bars protruding up or down from a centreline, as shown below. A series of bars that are below the centreline and shortening, or bars above the centreline that are lengthening, indicate a rising price trend. Bars above the centreline that are shortening, or bars below the centreline that are lengthening, indicate a falling price trend. Possible entry points occur when bars below the centreline shorten and begin to become rising bars above the centreline. Possible exit points occur when bars above the centreline begin to shorten and become lengthening bars below the centreline.

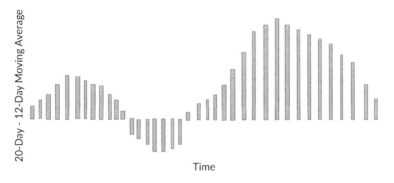

Histogram of average convergence and divergence (MACD)

The image below depicts the typical movements of the MACD. This indicator is particularly useful as it is known to be a leading indicator rather than a trailing one. As such it gives an early signal of changes in trend direction. As with all indicators, it is exactly that, an indicator rather than a 100% reliable signal. For this reason, traders tend to use a range of indicators to get a fix on what is happening.

Typical movements of the MACD

With this indicator, the darker line is a twenty-day moving average and the lighter line is a ten-day moving average. Crossovers indicate a change in price trend direction. The twenty-day being above the ten-day when prices are falling and below the ten-day moving average when prices are rising. Note the exponential moving average is used.

Stochastic oscillator

This indicator compares the price of a stock to the range of its prices over set periods of time. Traders use both short (fast) and long (slow) time periods. The output is a score of between 1 and 100. A low score below 20 that moves above 20 is seen as an indicator of a trend changing from downwards towards upward movement. Similarly, a score of above 80 that falls below 80 is an indicator of the start of a downward trend.

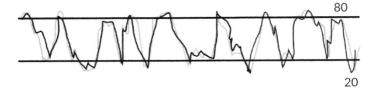

Stochastic Oscillator

In the indicator above, the dark oscillating line is the more responsive 'fast' oscillator and the grey line is the less responsive 'slow' oscillator. The strongest indication is when both the fast and slow oscillators have crossed the 80 or 20 lines and have turned in the opposite direction, forming a 'v'.

Candlestick patterns

A large element of technical analysis is the observation and interpretation of 'patterns' made up from series of candlesticks. A simple run of candlesticks with successively higher high-price points and higher low-price points is an upward trend. A series of candlesticks with lower high-price points and lower low-price points is a downward trend. Technical analysts take this much further. There are many different candlestick patterns. Here we can only look at a few examples, which are most often taken notice of by the extraordinary investment clubs.

There are many books about candlesticks, just as there are about indicators. As with the approach of the clubs to indicators, they generally use just a few of those available.

Gaps

A gap occurs when there is no overlap between the candlestick of one day and that of the next. The second candlestick involved could be higher or lower than the first candlestick, as shown below.

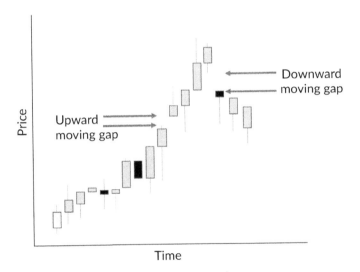

Around 80% of such gaps close within a fairly short period of time. The market doesn't like gaps! Traders mainly use gaps to assist in choosing entry and exit points for trades. If closing a gap within a reasonable period looks like a bit of a stretch, they may use the opening point of the gap as a target instead of the closing point as a trade exit target.

Doji

Dojis indicate a change in direction of a trend. The Doji occurs when there is equal buying and selling activity around the stock. It takes the form of a cross. The body of the candlestick is almost nonexistent and the wicks above and below it are usually fairly short and of about equal length. The market can't decide whether the price should be rising or falling, as demand is equal.

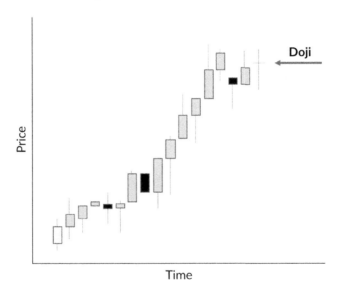

The Doji

As with all the trend lines, indicators and candlestick patterns, the Doji needs to be taken as part of a pattern of behaviour, with several others supporting any trading decisions taken on the back of its occurrence.

Falling knife

A 'falling knife' occurs when a stock price has a sharp downward drop. The expression comes from the phrase: 'Don't try to catch a falling knife'. It warns traders that they need to wait, to let the price 'bottom out', before they consider trading it. The term isn't precise; there is no test that says a price fall is or isn't a falling knife. It is usually obvious, though.

Sometimes, falling knives hit false support levels. The fall looks as though it's over, as the strong downward candlestick is followed by an upward one. Therefore, traders want to see several days of data to get confirmation that the knife (or, rather, the price) has stopped falling.

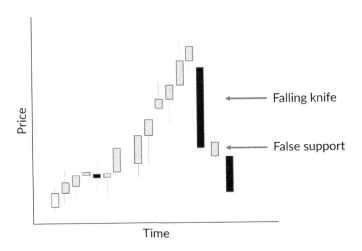

Falling knife

Forecasts

Starting with the long list of about 200 stocks, with charts and indicators it can take less than twenty minutes to visually eliminate those stocks that don't look as though they are at the start of an uptrend. The club traders usually end up with between sixty and eighty stocks that have most – but not necessarily all – indicators predicting an increasing price trend. The sixty to eighty identified stocks may have entry points that look reasonable, but there are no guarantees.

The traders also need to look at potential exit points. A $40-priced stock that is turning from a downward to an upward trend won't interest them unless they expect the subsequent price increase to be significant. To the clubs, the idea of significant is having at least a 25% price gain potential. They usually see a range of potential increases between around 5% and 100% or more, but ignore anything less than 25%. This is the first of three forecasts used by the clubs to determine their view of how prices may move.

Forecasts are exactly that – forecasts. As such, they won't all be correct all the time. The clubs normally only rely on around 50% of the forecast increase for each stock price. News events such as the pandemic can seriously change outcomes, as can overall market changes and many other factors. That said, there needs to be a target in mind as a starting point. Here are the forecasts that the clubs use.

Club member forecasts

For the first forecast, each weekend the members, trad-ers or a volunteer trawl through the long list of stocks to identify those that appear to be at good entry price points. They then look at possible resistance points that are likely future turning points and consider the 'character' of each stock to get an idea of how quickly or slowly it tends to move. They are most interested in forecasting movement over the short term, which to the clubs is around three to six months.

Using the forecast prices, a percentage potential increase is calculated and the stocks are ranked from highest to lowest percentage increase. The highest increase is provisionally the number-one most-wanted stock, the second-highest is the second most-wanted, and so on. Where the increase is below around 25%, the stock is eliminated from the candidate list. Candidates ranked below around fiftieth to sixtieth on the list are also eliminated.

Value Line eighteen-month target

The clubs use the Value Line eighteen-month medium-term forecast as their second forecast. Remember, Value Line have about an 85% accuracy rate. This forecast provides a range of their lowest and highest price expectations and a midpoint price. The clubs use the midpoint price forecast. Once more, they calculate the percentage increases and rank the stocks, and then eliminate those with less than a 25% forecast increase – those that are below the fiftieth to sixtieth rankings in the forecast.

The Value Line medium-term forecast is also used to provide a short-term reality check. If, according to Value Line, a stock is expected to rise by $9.00 over the next eighteen months, it may be reasonable for it to rise by $3.00 (or a third of $9.00) over the coming six months. If the club forecast looks different from this, they look again more closely at what they expect to happen and adjust their short-term forecast accordingly.

Value Line three- to five-year target

The exercise is repeated one more time using the long-term Value Line three- to five-year forecast to get the third forecast. Value Line don't provide a midpoint on this forecast, just their upper and lower price expectations. The clubs have found it useful to calculate and use the midpoint price of the Value Line expectations.

Once again, stocks forecast to rise by less than 25% and those ranked below the top fifty to sixty are removed from the candidate list. The elimination process is a little more forgiving on rankings for the third forecast if the club and medium-term rankings look good. It is not seen as reasonable to eliminate prospective stocks that have good short- to medium-term forecasts just because the long-term forecast is a little below par.

Most wanted

At the end of this process, there is normally a list of around fifteen stocks that each rank in the top fifty to sixty highest forecast growth percentages across all three forecasts. Now the clubs have a shortlist!

If shares were being simply bought to hold, the selection work would be just about complete. The shortlisted candidates would be looked at for affordability in club forecast ranked order. To ensure trading, the stocks wouldn't give the account involved too many shares in a single company or industrial sector. Finally, the list is considered in terms of current news, preferences, etc. For example, some clubs may have an objection to particular stocks or sectors, such as airlines, which may be removed after discussion. The traders then start buying the remaining candidate stocks in batches of 100 shares, working their way down the list.

Because the clubs trade options, there is more work to do. Affordability and diversification are still considered. Available option premiums, how much stock buying power (SBP) a trade would use and the cost of protecting the trades also need to be considered. These factors will each be covered later in the book.

The table below is an extract from a weekly updated data sheet used by the extraordinary investment clubs to identify possible trades. The percentage figures are the forecast percentage price increases. The club forecast is based on a six-month outlook, while the Value Line forecast is their eighteen-month midpoint price view. The two columns to the right show the ranking of the percentage increases relative to the full list of stocks.

Extract from a weekly extraordinary investment club data analysis exercise

Stock	Club forecast % rise	Value Line 18-month % rise	Most-wanted club short-term ranking	Most-wanted Value Line 18-month ranking
KGC	46.34%	37.80%	20	8
CDE	72.41%	24.14%	5	23
ERIC	39.47%	41.05%	31	3
WDC	42.09%	28.45%	28	28
WBD	117.54%	18.13%	1	7
RAMP	48.53%	28.56%	19	21
JBLU	61.29%	35.79%	9	14
SNBR	54.54%	32.23%	15	19
NMIH	38.57%	21.34%	33	36
M	37.67%	32.75%	35	11
AMKR	30.79%	24.80%	50	25
CAKE	27.28%	29.87%	58	17
AEO	33.44%	36.17%	41	9
ST	38.11%	19.73%	34	54
CTRN	32.32%	41.51%	46	5

Bear in mind, more stocks have been removed from the list for reasons other than their ranking. Removal could be because of low premiums, high SBP usage or the imminence of earnings announcements, for example.

Note that all the entries are judged by both the clubs and Value Line to be in their top 50 out of the 200 stocks in the long list, in terms of the percentage by which they are forecast to increase in price. Note also that the stocks are not listed in the order in which they rank for percentage rises in price on either forecast. The order has instead been determined by the annualised return on capital employed (ROCE – the return on SBP used) using specific put option strike prices, expiration month choices and premium levels.

News and earnings

No matter how proficient anyone becomes in forecasting, their output can be blown off course by news events. In the long term, it is mainly profits that drive prices in stock markets. However, news and sentiment play a large part in causing short- to medium-term price movements.

News events often provide opportunities to buy sound stocks at bargain prices. Major events such as the onset of a pandemic, recession, war and many others can push overall market prices up or down with the effects not necessarily evenly distributed between industrial sectors or companies in those sectors. To date, the overall market trend has always recovered its upward momentum, even if it has left individual sectors or companies battered, bruised or even dead!

Some news events occur suddenly and can't easily be predicted. Natural disasters or other catastrophes could fall into this category. The extraordinary investment club approach to trading tends to give a cushion in these circumstances. The clubs promise to buy stocks at a discount and can alter their promises, changing the price or date involved.

Other news events arrive after a period of uncertainty. For example, for months it was unclear whether President Putin would invade Ukraine. We knew it was a possibility but there was a lot of uncertainty. Market sentiment doesn't like uncertainty, so stock prices began to fall. Once the uncertainty clears, prices frequently rise, even if the worst news expected happens. We saw this once the wars in Iraq started. The invasion of Ukraine didn't end the uncertainty because it created other unknowns such as increasing inflation and shortages of fuel and grain. However, the uncertainty was working its way through and, at the time of writing, stock prices are recovering strongly.

Not all news occurs suddenly or after a period of uncertainty. Some news comes around like clockwork. This includes the publication of economic news, employment figures, inflation rates and similar. Many such announcements can move prices, albeit usually temporarily. Often, the reaction of the market to such news announcements seems illogical. Good news on employment, for example, can see stock prices fall! For this reason, the clubs don't look for short-term trading gains based on such announcements.

News also comes from the publication of company results or earnings, usually quarterly. The market is fickle regarding the effect of company results on stock prices. If results are even slightly better or worse than the forecasts of analysts, the market can over-react. The clubs can profit from such overreactions, but it is usually better to stand clear until results have been announced because the effects on price are so unpredictable.

Before undertaking any trade, the traders of the extraordinary investment clubs check out earnings. They look first for the expected publication date of the quarterly results of the stocks they are considering. If the dates fall within a week or two of the trade date, they take particular care and consider what the professional analysts expect the results to be. If most analysts have a mainly positive view – or even positive to neutral – the traders will be more inclined to go ahead. If the analysts' views have a significant proportion of negative predictions in them, the traders may hold off. In some cases, they will hold back until the earnings are announced and then take advantage of the price fall that may result.

Proximity to expiration date

A further influence on trading decisions is how close an option expiration date is. Option premiums reduce faster as their expiration date approaches. In addition, expiration dates tend to hold prices down until after expiry. This is particularly the case when a stock price is close to a strike price. A strike price is one that the promises inherent in option trades allow options to be bought or sold in respect of. It seems to be the case that allowing prices to climb above strike prices at expiration causes more work for the brokers. If the price does rise above a strike price, the brokers must find buyers and sellers to match the resulting trades. This effect shouldn't be overestimated, but it certainly is a real, observable effect.

The rise and fall of individual stock prices frequently follow a pattern of falls for two weeks before monthly option expiration dates and rises for two weeks after expiration dates. Obviously, there are many exceptions, but the phenomenon is real.

TRADER PROFILE

Lucia came to the United Kingdom from Slovenia and works as a management consultant in the health sector.

She is passionate about the environment and supports environmental projects including extensive tree planting programmes. She would like to be financially free to allow her to have wider lifestyle choices such as being able to devote more time to these projects. Lucia is also aware that she started building her pension at least a decade later in life later than most people and of the effects this could have.

Lucia is now on course to achieve her plan and to have a pension that will support what she considers to be a good lifestyle. At the current trajectory, with her own trading and being a member of an extraordinary investment club, Lucia will reach her objective in five to seven years.

Lucia's parents are ageing and increasingly ailing. Given where they are and where she is, there is a possibility that her life plan may have to alter to accommodate her parents' needs. Whatever other effects this may have, she is confident that it won't disrupt her financial wellbeing.

Always interested in putting something back, Lucia is now the treasurer of one of the investment clubs and supports its members by undertaking that role.

Summary

Technical analysis is a big subject. In short, it is the use of stock chart candlestick patterns and indicators to forecast price movements.

There are a bewildering number of both candlestick patterns and indicators, and they all have avid supporters. The extraordinary investment clubs use only a handful of each; however, they do take notice of those covered in this chapter.

At best, technical analysis gives varying degrees of probability that a stock price is going to behave in a particular way. The stock market can be unpredictable and frequently confounds any attempt to forecast its movements.

The extraordinary investment clubs maintain a healthy disrespect for forecasts, no matter what they are based on or who they come from. In the minds of the members:

1. Forecasts can be used, but can't be wholly relied upon. They usually work on the basis that a stock price will get to about halfway towards the forecast figure.

2. They use a forgiving trading methodology that does not rely on accurate forecasts.

The last paragraph may appear to be at odds with the earlier words indicating that Value Line forecasts are around 85% accurate. Value Line forecasts are generally correct but they look at least eighteen months into the future, they offer what is sometimes a wide range of possible outcomes and they get revised as time moves forward. The trades that the clubs undertake tend to have a three-to-six-month timespan. All of that said, the ultimate objective of the clubs is to own a portfolio of shares that are forecast to increase in value substantially over the longer term. Therefore, they do like the stocks they trade to be those with the highest long-term forecast increases according to Value Line.

In closing Part One, I would also say that the extraordinary investment clubs require lists of stocks that are good to trade, both to find new stocks to enter trades with and as part of maintaining their existing portfolios of trades. If you intend to trade on a small scale, it is possible to assess individual stocks, rather than a list, for their suitability. Even without Value Line it is possible to get much of the required information through web searches and by looking at the investor pages of the companies involved. This is not ideal as it doesn't allow the ranking of opportunities in terms of how good the trades are expected to be. It does, though, obviate the need to buy in research. That said, a small investment into one of the extraordinary investment clubs can give everything needed to compare stocks easily as often as members want to.

Part One Summary

You have now reached a major milestone. Hopefully, you are already beginning to see the power of what the extraordinary investment clubs do.

So far, we have identified good stock markets to operate within and have all the information needed to produce a watchlist and to convert that into a ranked list of opportunities to trade. You have also had an opportunity to 'meet' a handful of the members through their trader profiles, and to get an understanding of the varied circumstances and motivations they have. You will meet more members as you continue through the book.

The analyses that the clubs go through may seem daunting – it may even look as though there is a degree of analysis paralysis! Be assured that it takes just a couple of hours each week to get it done.

The whole of Part One has been about identifying stocks to trade. Of course, that is pointless unless they are traded. Some 99% of traders don't get as far as you now have. Most trade without a process for properly identifying good stocks to trade, let alone entry and exit points. I believe that only around 5% of those who trade do so using options. Of those, as many as 95% do it without training, education – or much success!

In Part Two you will be introduced to what I believe to be the most powerful trading methodology that is available to home-based traders. It is more power-ful and leads to more success than most professional traders could even dream of. That is in part because of scale. As mentioned earlier, the big guys can't do what the clubs do. So, get set, open your mind and let's get into the trading methodology.

PART TWO
MAKING MONEY

In Part One we concentrated on constructing a watchlist of good stocks to trade. In Part Two we will be seeing how the extraordinary investment clubs put the watchlist to work with actual trading. We will look at how they enter and close trades but also at how trades are maintained and how the clubs react to unexpected price increases and falls.

This book was written in the summer of 2022. The war in Ukraine was raging, petrol prices were costing close to £100 per tank for a typical family car, and gas and energy prices were rising at an unprecedented rate. Costs were rising across the board and the disruption of raw materials supply was more than starting to bite. Recession was anticipated across Europe and the USA as well as in the UK.

Many of the stocks traded by the clubs operate globally and prices were falling to reflect their operating climates. Even companies not directly affected by these events were seeing cost increases and falling demand. McDonald's increased the price of a Big Mac for the first time in fourteen years. The USA didn't have a grain shortage, but the economy there was suffering from higher energy prices and many indirect effects.

The watchlist of the extraordinary investment clubs reflected the above circumstances. For example, many retail and leisure stocks were at bargain prices. While that is great for entering trades, the clubs needed to be careful not to let their portfolios become overrepresented by any one stock or industrial sector – safety first.

Throughout Part Two we will be working with the watchlist given in the table below. This is a real list; it was generated in the first week of June 2022. By the time you come to read this, the list will be completely out of date. Do not use any of the information as a basis on which to trade the stocks on the watchlist. The contents are given purely for educational reasons and do not represent advice to trade any of the stocks.

Here is the list we will be working with; all the stocks are listed on the NYSE.

Company	Ticker symbol	Business sector
Alibaba Group	BABA	Software & IT services
Altice Inc.	ATUS	Telecommunications
American Eagle Outfitters	AEO	Speciality retail
AngloGold Ashanti	AU	Metals & mining
Bed Bath & Beyond Inc.	BBBY	Speciality retail
Big Lots Inc.	BIG	Diversified retail
Blackberry Ltd.	BB	Software & IT services
Carnival Corp.	CCL	Hotel & entertainment
Citi Trends Inc.	CTRN	Speciality retail
Dish Network Corp.	DISH	Media & publishing
eBay Inc.	EBAY	Software & IT services
Ericsson	ERIC	Comms & networking
Foot Locker	FL	Speciality retail
Fossil Group Inc.	FOSL	Textiles & apparel
Jet Blue Airways Corp.	JBLU	Passenger transport
Liveramp Holdings Inc.	RAMP	Software & IT services
Millerknoll Inc.	MLKN	Prof & commercial services
NCR Corp. Inc.	NCR	Software & IT services
NMI Holdings Inc.	NMIH	Insurance
Ollie's Bargain Outlet Inc.	OLLI	Diversified retail
Rent-a-Center Inc.	RCII	Speciality retail
Sleep Number Corp.	SNBR	Household goods

Continued

Company	Ticker symbol	Business sector
The Gap Inc.	GPS	Speciality retail
The Hain Celestial Group Inc.	HAIN	Food & tobacco
The Walt Disney Co.	DIS	Media & publishing
TTEC Holdings Inc.	TTEC	Software & IT services
US Steel Corp.	X	Metals & mining
Warner Bros. Discovery Inc.	WBD	Media & publishing

FOUR

How The Clubs Trade

The extraordinary investment clubs get paid for promising to buy shares. The clubs enjoy price appreciation and dividends on the shares that they accumulate and also get paid for promising to sell shares. They build a significant portfolio of stocks while keeping hold of their cash! The key to all of this is the fact that the clubs trade stock options.

Not all the above gain generators are open to every trader. Some trade types require a minimum account value. Some also require the account holder to have a level of knowledge and experience. The training that the extraordinary investment club members go through has satisfied the trading platform operators to a degree that they can undertake any buy, sell or option trade, if the account being traded meets the minimum value rules given below.

All amounts in US Dollars:

- Between 500 and 2,000: buy and sell shares

- Between 2,000 and 25,000: buy and sell shares and sell covered calls

- Between 25,000 and 100,000: buy and sell shares, sell covered calls and sell naked puts

- Above 100,000: every trade possible

Buy and hold

Trading accounts – at least the trading accounts that the clubs use – can be opened with just a minimum of $500 in them. However, with an account value below $2,500 it is normally the case that call options can't be traded. The holders of such accounts can only buy, hold and sell shares and collect dividends.

That's not a problem. All the work done so far in respect of finding high-quality stocks that represent great value and are available at good entry-point prices is still valid. The account holder has a bit of work to do to get the account value up to $2,500. Then they can sell covered calls, as described below.

Before buying any stock there are three practical matters to consider. Note: the following three factors also apply to the buying and selling of options.

Commission

Buying (or, for that matter, selling) shares is not usually a free service. The institutions behind the trade, brokers, market makers and others want paying for their work. The brokers take payment by collecting commission. This is usually a fixed amount per trade. With the Alpha Plan platform, the extraordinary investment clubs currently pay $11.95 per trade. This applies to buy and sell trades, irrespective of the number or value of the shares involved. As the number of shares being traded increases, the significance of the commission falls. With 100 shares bought at $10 each, commission represents 1.195%. If 1,000 shares were bought at $50 each, the $11.95 would represent just 0.0239%. The commission rate on option trades, currently at $14.95 per trade, is a little higher.

Spreads

Stock and option prices are always quoted as two prices: a bid and an ask price. The ask price is always the higher of the two and is the price we pay when we buy stock or options. The bid price is always lower and is the price we get when we sell stock or options.

The difference between the bid and ask prices is known as 'the spread'. Effectively this is a mark-up and therefore a cost to us. The spread income is the income source of the market makers. Spreads vary, depending on market conditions, the stock or option involved, current levels of volatility and the volume of stock or options being traded in respect of each company. The clubs only trade the stocks of large, well-traded companies. There are several good reasons for this, and one of them is that we want to be sure there is a good market when we come to sell such assets. A high volume of trades and tight spreads are a good indication of this.

Limit and market orders

A limit order is one where the trader gives the broker the maximum price they are prepared to pay when buying and the minimum price they are prepared to accept when selling. Once the order is placed, the limit price can be changed if the trade has not actually triggered. This is important because it allows minds to be changed and prices to be negotiated.

Limit orders can be placed to be cancelled if not filled by the end of the trading day or left to run until cancelled by the trader. Therefore, scope exists to renegotiate prices up until an order is filled.

A market order is one where the trader accepts whatever price the market dictates. The clubs virtually never use market orders as they give brokers too much power over what the price will be.

Negotiation

Most traders don't realise that it is possible to negotiate stock and option prices. The clubs regularly negotiate lower prices when buying and higher prices when selling.

As indicated above, negotiation is done through limit orders. An example that is often achieved is for the trade to trigger a better price than first quoted when buying a limit order that had been set towards the lower end of a spread and had increased until the trade occurred. For sell trades, the limit price is set towards the top of the spread and brought down until the trade is filled. Of course, in either case the order can be cancelled if it doesn't trigger at a price that the trader is happy with.

Records

Trading platforms show the prices paid for stocks within our portfolios. If more than one batch of shares is bought, the platform will show the average price paid. However, if stock was put to the account through the sale of a put option, the price paid may not show. In such circumstances, the broker can be contacted to enter the price manually. Trading platforms also have an area where the history of all orders placed is shown. In addition, the back office clearing house involved will show full details.

When an account is only used for buying and selling stocks, the trading platform record may be perfectly adequate. As things get more complicated it is beneficial to keep detailed records. It is a good idea to start recording all transactions on a spreadsheet right from the start.

Buying shares

Consulting our watchlist, the top ten forecast increases in stock price are:

Stock	Current price	Forecast price	Percentage increase
BBBY	$7.12	$30.00	321.25%
WBD	$14.86	$60.00	303.77%
CTRN	$25.39	$100.00	293.86%
CCL	$11.05	$30.00	171.49%
GPS	$9.47	$25.00	163.99%
SNBR	$37.32	$94.00	151.88%
AEO	$11.92	$30.00	151.68%
FOSL	$6.50	$15.00	130.77%
ATUS	$10.00	$23.00	130.00%
DISH	$20.08	$45.00	124.10%

Unfortunately, the small-scale trader may not be able to start at the top of the list with the trades that have the most potential. Some stocks have far higher prices than others. Warren Buffett's Berkshire Hathaway currently trades at around $429,819.44 per share. However, there are plenty of good stocks at below $10 or even below $5 each.

Based on the analysis, the Bed Bath & Beyond (ticker symbol: BBBY) stock was selected. This stock was trading well below its value and has a track record that makes $30 a reasonable price expectation.

For both simulated and live trading accounts, traders need 'margin'-type accounts to trade options. Margin = borrowing! Although they need that type of account, they won't actually be borrowing. Quite the opposite, they will gain interest on their cash as another income source.

Note: when buying shares, do so in a round number of hundreds, for example 100, 200 or 500 shares. That is because options are traded in batches of 100 shares, referred to as contracts. One contract equals 100 shares.

When shares are owned, the extraordinary investment clubs take advantage of the fact that prices don't move in straight lines. For example, when a stock doubles in price – and there are plenty of them that do – it is forecast to go from, say, $20 to $40, which is a 100% increase. This may take several rises and falls to reach the forecast. In other words, it zigs and zags rather than going in a straight line.

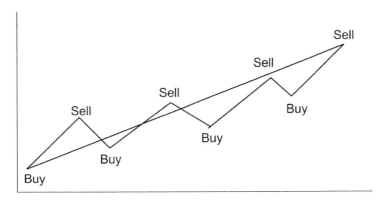

Typically, there is 70% more gain available using repeated buying and selling rather than buy and hold.

If a trader could repeatedly buy at the low points and sell at the high points of its journey, they would normally see an increase of an extra 70% in gains.

This is yet another example of how small-scale traders can do something that the big guys simply can't. Imagine the chaos if Warren Buffett tried to buy and sell his 10% stake in Coca-Cola every month or so! Even with the cream of graduate talent and super-computers, there are things that major investors can't do, purely because of scale.

Most trading platforms, including Alpha Plan, provide free simulated accounts and training guides on how to use them.

The account is growing, what next?

Depending on the opening value of the account, the objective at this stage is to build the account value to a level above $2,500, or to above $25,000 in value if you can start with more. In either case, getting above $2,500 brings the opportunity to sell covered call options. We call this renting out our shares.

Let's now assume that our trader owns some shares and has built the account value to over $2,500. The account can now be used to trade covered call options, so let's see what they are.

Selling covered calls

The best way I have found to explain selling covered calls is to use an example from the world of home buying – a world more familiar to most people than options trading. Think of a young couple going off to a new housing development to buy a house. They pick out a plot and for a small fee of, say, £200, they reserve a house. They then usually have a period of about three months to arrange to pay for the property.

From the builder's perspective, she has sold the couple an option. If the couple are willing and able to complete the deal, they can buy the agreed property on the agreed plot for an agreed price on or before an agreed date. Alternatively, the couple can walk away, but they will lose £200 if they do so.

In a covered call transaction, the clubs act as the builder. They own shares and undertake to sell them to a potential buyer at an agreed price on or before an agreed date if the potential buyer wants to complete the transaction. The buyer will have paid the club, normally more than 5% of the price that the shares will be 'called' away from them at. The club keeps the 5% or more, irrespective of the offer to sell being taken up or not. If the offer is taken up, then they get the agreed sale price too.

Note that this type of trade is called a 'covered call'. That is because the trader owns the shares that are being offered for sale and can deliver them if the potential buyer 'calls' them away – that is, buys them.

Let's use Bed Bath & Beyond as an example of selling covered calls. While it is possible to sell a covered call as soon as shares are owned, normally the price is allowed to increase to its next natural resistance point before the trade is undertaken.

Take it that a club owns 500 shares in Bed Bath & Beyond. Assume it is currently at a point of resistance. In other words, the price is expected to fall a little as part of its zigzag journey up towards the price we see as its medium-term high. The current price is $7.12.

The trader now visits the option chain section of the trading platform. Ideally, they will find a call option at a strike price that expires in a month or so. The trader wants to promise to sell the shares at a price, known as the 'strike price', that is higher than the price paid for the shares. The income received for making the promise to sell is called the 'premium' and the end date of the life of the promise is called the 'expiration date'. The expiration dates used by the club are normally on the third Friday of each month. The alternatives for the third Friday of July 2022 expiring covered calls, offered on 10 June 2022, were:

1. **$0.91 per share in premium for the $8.00 strike price**

   If the stock price remains below $8.00, the club will keep the stock and keep the $0.91. If the stock ends up above $8.00 the shares will, almost certainly, be sold, called away, for $8.00, and the club will also keep the $0.91 as well as the difference between the price paid for the shares and the sale price.

   This means not 5% but $0.91/$7.12 = 12.78% if the stock is retained and $8.00 − $7.12 + $0.91 = $1.79, or 25.14%, if the shares are called away. All these prices were 'on the day'. You can see why traders don't always wait for the stock price to rise before selling a covered call.

2. **$0.68 per share in premium for the $9.00 strike price**

   If the stock price remains below $9.00, the trader will keep the stock and keep the $0.68. If the stock ends up above $9.00 the shares will probably be sold for $9.00, and the trader will also keep the $0.68 and the difference between the purchase and sale prices of the stock.

   That means, again not 5% but $0.68/$7.12 = 9.55% if the stock is retained and $9.00 − $7.12 + $0.68 = $2.56, or 35.95%, if the shares are called away.

   Remember, the call option is set to expire in just a month or so. Commission has not been taken into account and there was no negotiation.

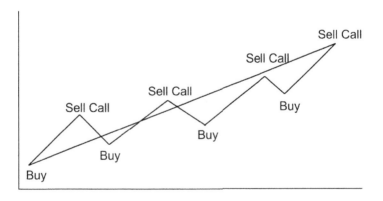

The choice is yours. These are two alternatives from many that are available, but they are typical of how the extraordinary investment clubs trade covered calls and do so well.

Bear in mind, we have the potential to do this twelve times per year. That would allow the modification and improvement of the model sketched above to something like this:

Checking out the premiums for August covered calls, the $8.00 strike price pays $1.35 and the $9.00 strike price pays $0.95.

Time needs to be considered. The July covered call options expire in 32 days compared to the August options, which expire in 67 days.

Comparing the two $8.00 calls, we get $0.91 / 32 days = $0.028 per day for July and $1.35 / 67 days = $0.020 per day for the August call. Effectively, the July call pays 41% more than the July call and releases the shares earlier to be available to sell a new call on. In general, it is better to stay with closer expiration dates.

Some covered call options expire weekly, some monthly and others in each January. The extraordinary investment club's preference is to sell monthly options as they offer better premiums than the weekly expiring options. They also give more trading opportunities than would be had using the January expiring options. Note there are trading strategies specific to January expiring options. These are not currently used by the clubs.

Option premium levels are influenced by several factors. One of the more important factors is volatility. When the market or an individual stock is more volatile, premiums are higher than when volatility is low.

Once a covered call is sold, the stock is tied up. The trader can buy the promise back and sell a new one. This is referred to as 'rolling the call forward'.

As soon as a covered call is sold, the cash raised is available to traders to use within their trading accounts. With larger numbers of contracts, that can mean that traders sell calls and use the income to buy more shares, then sell more calls, perhaps even more than once.

The clubs only sell covered calls at strike prices that they are happy to sell the shares at. By selling covered calls when a trader believes the share price to be at a short-term peak, they increase the chance of retaining the shares and being able to repeat the exercise in the following month.

Most of the covered call options sold are at strike prices that are above the current price. These are called 'out of the money' (OTM) options. If, for example, a stock is trading at $10.00 per share, the trader could sell an OTM covered call sold against it at a strike price of, say, $12.00 per share.

Sometimes covered call options are sold at strike prices that are at or close to the current price of the stock. These are referred to as being 'at the money' (ATM).

It is also possible to sell call options at strike prices that are below the current share price. These are called 'in the money' (ITM) call options. The sale of ITM call options can be used to take profit from a trade before a price fall occurs. For example, a trader may buy a stock for $12.00, see it rise to $13.00 and expect it to fall back to $11.00. They may be able to anticipate the fall in price by selling an $11.00 strike price call, most likely for more than $2.00, thus staying in profit whatever the share price does.

Please note carefully: the extraordinary investment clubs only sell call options. They don't buy them unless they are buying them back.

As with stock purchases and sales, limit orders are used when selling or buying back call options. Different terms are given to the acts of buying and selling options. When a covered call is sold, the trade is called a 'sell to open' (STO) trade. If the call is bought back, it is through a 'buy to close' (BTC) order. It would be a good idea to practise these trades on your simulator before going anywhere near them on a live account.

Hopefully, you have now got a basic understanding of how covered call options work. Next, we turn our attention to where the clubs make most of their money. That is by selling put options.

Getting paid for promising to buy shares

To sell put options, an account value of at least $25,000 is required. Our first extraordinary investment club, Tees Traders, started with eight members each investing £100 per month. It took just nine months to build to the required $25,000 level. The investment in that period was £100 × 8 people × 9 months = £7,200. Of course, the investments came in month by month. The £800 that came in month one was available for the whole nine months. That which came in during month two was only available for seven months; that coming in during month three was available for six months, and so on. The point is that the club only had an average of £3,600 in the trading pot as new money and still got to the target. This was even more remarkable given that the club could not sell puts. It could only buy and sell stock and sell covered calls for part of the first nine months.

You are about to learn more about put options than 99.9% of traders know! The premise: the clubs promise to buy a set number of shares in a specific business whenever the seller wishes them to, up to an agreed (expiry) date, and to pay an agreed (strike) price in return for a sum of money (the premium).

Let's return to our old friend Bed Bath & Beyond, with its stock symbol BBBY. This time, the objective is to own 500 shares, but to a) get paid for buying them and b) push the commitment to buy them into the future.

The clubs normally sell put options that expire between three and six months into the future. Looking at BBBY, as of the middle of June 2022 there are put options available to sell that expire in July 2022, August 2022, November 2022, January 2023 and January 2024. August is too soon, given what's happened to retail stock recently, and 2024 is too far away. Going out to 2024 would tie capital (and SBP) up for a long time. The choice is going to be between options that expire in November 2022 and January 2023.

The club forecast, and those of Value Line, are telling us that the BBBY stock price should get to between $30.00 and $35.00 from its current $7.12 within the next six to eighteen months.

If a put with a strike price at the high end of our expectations is sold, there will be a strong possibility that the stock will be put to the club. Although they would get a large premium, it would probably just reflect the difference between the current price and the strike price. They would end up owning the share without it having much scope to increase in price. In addition, the forecast could be wrong by a large degree.

Instead, they will choose a much lower strike price, which is more likely to be reached by the stock and carries a discount within it. The November 2022 $11.00 strike price put carries a premium, at present, of $5.30. With the current stock price at $7.12, there is a discount of $7.12 − ($11.00 − $5.30) = $1.42 built in − that is almost 13%.

The January 2023 $11.00 strike price put has a premium of $5.75, which means a discount of $1.87 or 17%. The November expiry date is 158 days away, giving an annualised return of (13% / 158 days) × 365 days = 30%, while the January 2023 expiry date is 221 days away, giving an annualised return of (17% / 221) × 365 = 28%. Given this, and the wish to keep reusing capital, the club would opt for the closer date.

When a trader sells a put option at a strike price that is higher than the current price, they are selling an ITM option. This is the opposite to a covered call option where a strike price is above the current price, which is an OTM option. The term for put options with strike prices at or close to the current stock price is, like in a covered call, termed 'at the money' (ATM). For put options, an OTM trade occurs when the strike price is below the current strike price.

The premium income from put sales goes into the cash of trading accounts but shows as a negative amount. It isn't available to reuse immediately, as it is in the case of a covered call option. The cash slowly moves into the usable cash value of the account as the option price falls and/or expires.

TRADER PROFILE

Andy is a self-employed plumber and gas engineer. He is doing well with his business but realises that his ability to exchange time for money won't always be what it is at present. The work involved can be heavy, dirty and uncomfortable. His back and knees are already suffering. He believes that he will need to slow down at a relatively young age but was worried that doing so would seriously impact his income.

The amount of money he would need to put into a conventional pension fund to maintain a good standard of living from his mid-fifties was prohibitive. The level of savings needed would seriously impact his current lifestyle. He has a family to support and a hefty mortgage to cover. Andy is also aware that any illness serious enough to stop him working for a significant period would be a financial disaster.

Andy joined one of the extraordinary investment clubs and makes regular, affordable contributions. He is now well on track to being able to pay off his mortgage and retire in around ten years or so, if he needs or wants to. He is confident that, even if he had to stop work after around five years, he could afford to live with a much lower income supplemented by his investment club returns.

Summary

In this chapter you were introduced to the world of option trading. You saw some remarkable premiums being paid for promises to sell or buy stock through covered call and put options.

You learned that the extraordinary investment clubs only sell covered call options and use STO trades for this. They only ever buy call options to close a trade and use BTC trades for that purpose. Similarly, they only enter put STO trades and only buy puts to close existing put trades through BTC trades.

The worst that can happen when puts are sold is that shares get put to the clubs at prices that they were happy to pay anyway. Money can be made by buying put trades. Lots of traders do this – however, the extraordinary investment clubs don't as they consider it to be too risky.

The examples of option trades given above are not unusual, they are typical. The extraordinary investment clubs are constantly undertaking similar trades.

Most of the money the clubs make, especially in the early years, comes from selling puts. I have therefore dedicated the next chapter to the possible outcomes of put trades.

FIVE

Possible Put Trade Outcomes

In the introduction to this book, I used the analogy of a special dice that produced a winning number no matter which face it landed on. That was a reference to the six outcomes we see as possibilities from the sale of a put option, as described in Chapter 4.

Some of the outcomes possible from selling puts through STO trades are standalone. Others depend on a second, supplementary trade being placed at the same time as the put is sold. The extraordinary investment clubs refer to these supplementary trades as 'lid' trades because they can cap the outcome of the trade. The lid trades are set through limit orders and don't always trigger. However, when they do, they guarantee that the put sale will end in profit at the time of expiration. We start this chapter with an explanation of lid trades before going on to consider the six possible outcomes.

Lid orders

Every time the extraordinary investment clubs sell a put option, they also place a protective limit order that is intended to give them the right – but not the obligation – to sell the shares on at a price that is just one strike price below the strike price of the original put trade. In the BBBY example given in Chapter 4, the original strike price was $11.00. The next strike price down in that case would be $10.00. For some stocks, the intervals between strike prices are $0.50, $2.50 or even $5.00.

As a rule of thumb, lid order limit prices are no more than 10% of the premium that was paid for the put that was sold. In the BBBY example, the club would offer to pay around $0.50 to $0.75, depending on which alternative it took. Where the strike price intervals are wider, the limit price for the lid trade tends to be lower.

These trades are called lids because they cap off the potential for making a loss if they trigger. Assume the stock had been put to the club at $11.00 because the underlying stock price was down at, say, $5.00. If the lid was in place, the club could sell the stock for $10.00 per share, having had over $5.00 in premium income from it and having paid out just $0.50 or so for the lid. Once the lid is triggered, there is a guaranteed profit.

Furthermore, when a limit order triggers it releases capital in the form of buying power. In the BBBY example, exposure would be reduced from $11.00 per share to $1.50 per share if the $10.00 lid order triggered and the club had paid $0.50 for it. They would therefore have reduced their exposure by $9.50 per share. That, in turn, would release buying power to be recycled into more trades.

Outcome 1 – The club keeps the premium

Although the objective is to build a portfolio of shares in fundamentally sound companies bought at bargain prices that have great scope for price appreciation, the clubs don't always get to own the shares. Above, you saw a put sold that meant a club had promised to buy shares in Bed Bath & Beyond for $11.00 each. That was big of them as they, and Value Line, see the stock as having the potential to reach a price of $30.00.

Consider the situation where the stock price is at $11.01 at expiration date. Why would anyone want to sell the shares to the club for $11.00 when they can sell them to the market at $11.01 or they could just keep them. The club would not get the shares, but it would keep the $5.30 or $5.75 that it was paid as a premium for making the promise to buy.

This is not money for nothing!

1. The club took a risk that the stock price would fall. Admittedly, the stock price would have to have fallen to below $11.00 − $5.30 = $5.70 before the club incurred a loss and that was $1.42 or about 20% below the price of $7.12, which stood when the promise was sold, but hey, they took some risk!

2. The club gave the buyer of the promise comfort. The buyer of the put knew that the worst case for them was to sell the shares for $11.00. We don't know what they paid for them.

3. The club tied up capital. Every time a put is sold, the buying power is reduced in the trading account. Who knows what better alternative use may have been found for that capital had the club not done this deal?

We estimate that, over the last few years, around 80% of club put trades have ended in this way. That has made the clubs a lot of money.

Outcome 2 – The club acquires the shares

This outcome is straightforward. The shares are sold to the club at the agreed strike price. The members also keep the premium. The club can then, as the stock hits appropriate price points, start selling covered calls at higher price points that they are happy to sell the shares at. If the club decides to stay with the stock, it can sell more puts when it reaches low price points, that is at strong levels of support.

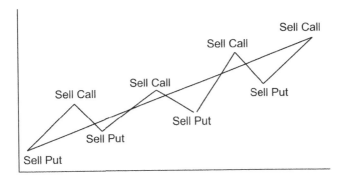

It is possible to benefit from put and call premiums in addition to price appreciation.

This outcome allows further development of the model used earlier through the addition of put sales to it.

Outcome 3 – Stock is put and sold through the lid

For outcome 3, we need to assume:

- That the lid order was triggered

- That the put we sold has not been closed

- That the stock price at expiration is lower than the strike of the lid

In these circumstances, the stock will be put to the club (possibly before the expiration date) and then automatically sold. The original premium should always be enough to cover the difference between the original strike price at which the stock is put and the strike price at which the stock will be sold, plus the cost of the lid.

For example, BBBY was put to the club at the $11.00 strike price with a premium of $5.30 per share and $0.50 was paid to buy the $10.00 strike price protective put – the lid. Outcome 3 would see the club gain $5.30 then pay $11.00 for the shares and $0.50 for the lid. The club would then sell the shares for $10.00, leaving it with $5.30 – ($0.50 + $1.00) = $3.80. (The $1.00 being the difference between the price paid for the shares and that at which they were sold.)

If the price of the stock stayed above $10.00, the shares would not be sold through the lid. It could occur, for example, that the price at expiration was $10.15. The club could choose to sell the shares at that price. They would be at least $0.15 further ahead than they would be selling them at $10.00 under the lid. They may even have saved the $0.50 outlay for the lid if the price being offered for it didn't get as low as $0.50.

Note that triggered lids expire at the same time as the puts they are protecting. In some cases, the stock may be put to the club before the expiration date, in which case they can use the lid to sell the shares on early. If they are happy to keep the shares, they may get the opportunity to sell the lid at a profit or even to use it to protect a new put sale on the same stock with the same expiration date and probably the same strike price as the original.

Outcome 4 – Stock is put, sold and replaced

When stock is put to a club at a strike price that is higher than the current price, they may choose to sell it immediately and get the trade into the black by selling a new put, if the premium they had been paid had not already done so.

For example, a club sold the $11.00 strike price BBBY put for a premium of $5.30 and the price fell from its starting point of $7.12 to, say, $5.00. They would then be in the red: they paid $11.00 for the shares and got $5.30 in income so are exposed at $11.00 − $5.30 or $5.70. With the price at $5.00 they are under water by $0.70.

However, they could sell the stock and a new put. If they got more than $0.70 in premium, they would be back in the black. The chances are that they could use a lower strike price put to do this. At the time of writing, they could have got a premium of $3.75 for an $8.00 strike price BBBY put, which would put them ahead by $3.05, ignoring commissions. They would then look at the closure alternatives on the new put in the same way as they did with the original put.

Outcome 5 – Put bought back before expiry

Puts that are sold can be bought back using a BTC order. If stock prices move up, the buy and sell prices of the put involved will fall. These prices also fall as the time left until expiration reduces.

Given the above, puts can be closed with a BTC trade with a lower cost than was received in premium, giving an overall gain.

There are two main reasons why clubs would want to BTC a put in profit:

1. They may just want the buying power back to use for another trade.

2. They may wish to avoid the cost of paying for the lid, particularly if the difference between the strike prices is high, like $5.00. In this case, the club may be better off closing a put trade and keeping 85% or more of the premium than they would be by allowing the stock to be sold through the lid.

When closing a put trade early, traders need to remember to also cancel the associated lid limit order or to sell the lid put off with a 'sell to close' (STC) order if it has already triggered.

Outcome 6 – Put bought back and replaced

The last of our six possible outcomes is one where a club has changed its mind, perhaps because the stock looks less likely to reach the strike price.

The club can buy their promise back through a BTC order, but that could leave them in the red if the price they needed to pay was higher than the premium they were paid. However, they could replace the put with a new one with a later expiration date and add to the premium that they already have.

At present, a club could buy back the November 2022 $11.00 strike price put for $5.40 having been paid $5.30 for it. They could then sell a January 2023 $11.00 put for $5.75. The cash movements would then be: + $5.30 − $5.40 + $5.75 = $5.65 leaving the club $0.35 better off and giving the stock some extra time to reach the $11.00 strike price.

The club could also use this technique to bring the strike price down. The January 2023 $9.00 strike price has a premium of $4.15. If they opted for this, their cash movements would be: + $5.30 − $5.40 + $4.15 = $4.05. While they would have a lower premium, they would also have a much lower exposure. Different combinations of expiration dates and premiums can be tested to find the one the club is most comfortable with.

TRADER PROFILE

Dan has done well through owning a small manufacturing business. He has accumulated what most people would consider to be a good cash pile – he is certainly wealthy in cash terms. However, the low rates of return offered by the financial institutions mean that he is relatively income poor. He has had to draw on his capital to meet living expenses instead of, as he had hoped, living off interest.

Dan, having seen how the extraordinary investment clubs trade, and the results, asked if a club could be developed that had income rather than capital growth as its central aim. This, I believed, was only possible if all the members of a club had the same objective and were prepared to take regular dividends – even if these were, in some cases, then reinvested as new money. A shout out across all of the extraordinary investment clubs quickly ascertained that there was interest, and a new club, the Quarterly Income Investment Club (QI), was formed.

It will take the first year or so of trading to prime things, but thereafter Dan and the other members of the QI Club expect to take a quarterly income. You can read more about the QI Club in Part Three.

Summary

There we have it; our special dice is in place. There are only six possible outcomes to our put trade, and they are all positive. Some have better and more immediate results than others. Normally, the worst case is that the clubs must keep rolling a trade forward for longer than expected. Even then, each roll brings an additional gain.

It is possible to roll trades forward forever if the clubs need to. Eventually, the additional gains would cover the cost of buying the stock, and the shares would be free! However, that is unlikely to be required in practice and it isn't something the clubs have ever needed to do.

What we have covered in this chapter is quite complicated. I advise caution and a lot of simulation before embarking on these trades. Even then, start in a small way.

The trades do become familiar with use, and a few simple calculations help. Members of the extraordinary investment club become used to these trades, having seen many of them. They have the advantage of training and coaching as well as just being able to check things through with other members before trading.

SIX
Other Trading Considerations

Up to this point we have covered the basic concepts that underpin how the extraordinary investment clubs select and trade stocks. To ensure that the concepts remain preeminent I have kept the detail to a minimum. However, before anyone considers embarking on the journey towards becoming a trader, they do need to understand and consider some ancillary concepts. This chapter concentrates on these important, not to be ignored, but still secondary matters.

The chapter is arranged in such a way that it covers the issues most closely related to trading first and then goes on to matters that relate to understanding how things are progressing. Some of the points made in this chapter are crucial to trading safely, while others are intended to help if things don't go to plan.

According to his blog, it was Warren Buffett who said, 'Rule No. 1: Never lose money. Rule No. 2: Never forget rule No. 1!'[7]

Using margin and overtrading are two of the biggest mistakes that traders make. None of the extraordinary investment clubs have fallen foul of either of these; however, there are inexperienced members who have done so with their own trading accounts. Thankfully, in every known case, they have been able to be helped to get out of trouble.

Margin

Quite rightly, many traders blanch at the word 'margin'. That is understandable, as using margin effectively means borrowing money to buy or maintain positions. That can be expensive and dangerous, and it is something the extraordinary investment clubs don't do. Imagine borrowing money to buy shares that subsequently halve or worse in value. A trader could end up owing a lot of money – more than the value of their account. They would soon be asked to put the shortfall into the trading account.

You will recall, though, that the clubs open margin bearing trading accounts – accounts that have a margin facility. We need a margin facility even though we

---

7   E Kirkhan, 'Genius things Warren Buffett says to do with your money', Yahoo Finance (1 May 2022), accessed 13 October 2022.

won't use it. When we promise to buy stock, we are promising to spend money in the future. Because of the margin facility, the promise can be to spend more money than has been deposited in the account. The promises are spread over several months and can be bought back, rolled forward, etc. Through such techniques, the clubs avoid using margin altogether.

They go further. Not only do they not use margin, but they also hang on to the cash they have deposited and only use the margin facility to trade. Because they have cash in their accounts, the clubs even get paid interest, albeit at less than brilliant rates.

Stock buying power and overtrading

The funds that margins make available to trade are shown in trading accounts as SBP. The amount of SBP available depends on the value of cash deposited and the strength of the portfolio of shares held in the account. Within the Alpha Plan trading account – and most others – SBP therefore emanates from two sources: 'real' cash and assets held.

If the account only had cash, the SBP would be double the value of that cash. Hence, trades can take place without using any actual cash. If the clubs promise to spend money rather than actually spending it, the cash remains in place.

Different stocks and options are allocated varying levels of strength by the brokers. Some stocks are treated like cash in terms of providing SBP. For example, a single share worth $10.00 would give another $10.00 of buying power. Other stocks are treated as having more strength and can attract three or four times the buying power of their current value. One of these with a current value of $10.00 could provide another $30.00 of buying power.

Let's not forget, though, a promise to spend actual hard cash in the future is being made when a put option is sold. If too many such promises are made, there is a danger that the value of the promises made will exceed the amount of money in the account.

To keep things safe, only a proportion of the SBP available is used. The extraordinary investment clubs keep their SBP at half the Net Liquid Value (NLV) of their account. Some traders opt to keep their use of SBP to no more than a third of the NLV, which is fine and a matter of personal choice. NLV is the value of the account if it was closed instantly. It includes the current value of any shares held and any cash, but the NLV is then reduced to reflect the cost of exiting any existing option trades. While NLV is good for keeping the account safe, it is not brilliant for gauging its real value. For this, the clubs use Left In Value (LIV), which is the current value of shares and withdrawable cash plus the value of yet-to-expire options.

Retaining a proportion of SBP provides a cushion against market pullbacks and bear markets. During such periods the level of SBP will fall below the level set by the trader. The whole point of setting the level is to give SBP scope to fall when market conditions reduce the account value.

The clubs class using too much SBP as overtrading and dangerous. Because stock prices are constantly moving up and down, even during a rising price trend, traders need to be prepared to see the value of their accounts fall as well as, in the medium to long term, increase.

Releasing stock buying power

If there has been overtrading or a major fall in prices, a trader may need to take action to keep the SBP positive. Not doing so will result in a margin call. A margin call is a request for more cash to be deposited in the trading account. Failure to respond quickly to the call will result in the brokers selling stock or options, of their choice, to return the SBP to a positive position.

Either to prevent SBP becoming negative or to get it back into the positive if it has gone negative, there are things that can be done, other than depositing more money. The most straightforward way to release SBP is to sell stock. The stock that is sold should be in profit! The clubs just don't accept any losses. If a choice is to be made as to which stock is to be sold, factors such as these should come into play:

- Which stocks are unencumbered by not having had covered calls sold against them?

- Can any call options that have already been sold be bought back at prices that are lower than the price they were sold for, to add stocks to the unencumbered list of possible sale candidates?

- Which stocks are closest to the exit price level that is planned for them?

- Which stocks will release the most buying power?

The last of these factors will require a bit of digging about to get a clear view of what positions can potentially release the most SBP. Generally, the facility exists in the back office of trading accounts to rank all current positions in terms of the SBP they are using. The list is normally headed as 'margin requirement'. This list allows traders to see exactly what SBP will be released by the sale of any stock.

Put options also use SBP. Therefore, closing a put trade through a BTC trade that has previously been opened through a STO trade will also release SBP. If there are put trades that can be bought back at lower prices than they were sold at, a gain will be had and some SBP released. The margin requirement ranking list will show what will be released from put trade closures, as well as from stock sales.

The next SBP-releasing technique may sound counterintuitive as it involves buying something! The purchase involved is of a put to act as a special lid.

As a rule, the clubs never buy puts other than as inexpensive protective lids bought through limit orders. To buy any put is to buy a promise from someone else to buy your shares at a set price within the time before the put expires. The put will expire worthless if it isn't sold.

Normally, clubs place Buy To Open (BTO) limit orders to buy lids on the puts they sell, to protect them and to ensure there is no scope for a loss position. Usually, the clubs offer to buy the lid at the next lower strike price below the put that was sold, through a limit order at a price that is just 10% or less of the premium income from the sale of the put being protected. The limit order triggers only if the price falls to the limit price.

To release SBP, the traders could buy a put for the same expiry date but at a much lower strike price. For example, we sold a $30.00 put for November and got a premium of $10.00 per share. The exposure is $30.00 − $10.00 = $20.00 per share. However, the market treats the position as being exposed to a promise to pay out $30.00 per share.

If a put is bought that gives the right to sell the stock at, say, $17.00, the market treats the exposure as being $30.00 − $17.00 = $13.00 per share. That would release the SBP of $17.00 × the number of shares involved in the trade × the factor applied by the market. Care needs to be taken to avoid buying the stock at $30.00 only to sell it for $17.00, giving a loss of $13.00 − $10.00 (the original premium) plus the cost of buying the $17.00 put. With that circumstance in mind, ownership of the $17.00 strike price put should be seen as temporary and the technique should be applied to an original put trade that has a long time to run to expiration.

The idea is to give the market time to rise so that the value of the account increases, thus allowing the secondary put to be sold, while keeping the SBP positive. Some degree of loss can be accepted on the sale of the SBP-releasing put if the trade remains in profit overall. In the above example, there is $10.00 of premium that can be used as a cushion against loss.

An alternative is to wait until a time near to the expiry date and then to roll the original and underpinning puts forward to a later expiration date for an additional credit. Probably the best outcome would be to sell the protective put when it is in profit and to replace it with a conventional lid once our SBP has recovered, as the market gets back to an upward trend.

Overtrading is a particular problem for smaller accounts. As frustrating as it may be, anyone trading accounts with a value of less than $75,000–$100,000 needs to be particularly wary. The $25,000 account value requirement to trade puts comes into play even after it has first been reached. If the NLV later falls below $25,000, the account will not be able to trade puts. If the account value has been over $25,000 and has not fallen too far below it, the broker can be asked to give a twenty-four-hour boost to the account value to allow puts to be bought to release buying power. The clubs don't trade puts until they are well above $25,000. When they first trade puts, they do so conservatively on a small scale.

Dollar cost averaging

The extraordinary investment clubs use dollar cost averaging a lot. The idea is simple. It involves buying stock at a lower price than that paid for stock in the same company, which was bought at a higher price. This reduces the average price paid for the stock.

For example, just three and a half months before writing this, shares in Bed Bath & Beyond (BBBY) were selling at $30.00. Today they are at $6.13. We are in a bear market triggered by the pandemic, the war in Ukraine, energy and grain price hikes, interest rate increases and whatever other bad news the media can drag up! However, the fundamentals of BBBY remain sound; they have plenty of cash, little debt, etc. We are confident that the stock will get back to at least $25.00, but it will take some time.

With $6.13 and $30.00 being so far apart, it is unlikely that covered calls could be sold at anywhere near strike prices of $30.00, so the alternatives appear to be to wait for a long time or to sell the stock at a loss. But surely $6.13 is an absolute bargain. The club traders believe so. If they had bought 1,000 shares at $30.00, they could buy more, such as another 1,000 at $6.13. Instead of owning 1,000 at an average price of $30.00 they would own 2,000 at an average price of (($30.00 × 1,000) + ($6.13 × 1,000))/2,000 = $18.07. They would have dollar cost averaged.

The number of additional shares taken at the lower price doesn't have to match the number originally owned. Depending on the overall exposure to the stock and the sector as a proportion of a portfolio, more or fewer additional shares could be bought. If an extra 2,000 had been purchased, the average price would have come down to $14.09. If only an extra 500 had been purchased, the average would have come down to $22.04.

Once some shares are owned at the lower price, they could be treated differently to the original batch, for example, covered calls could be sold on them or even buying and selling in the zigzag of price points to reach the price of the original stock owned.

Using puts to dollar cost average

It isn't necessary to own shares before dollar cost averaging starts. For example, assume no BBBY shares were purchased at $30.00 but a promise to buy some at that price, by selling a put, had been made. There will have been a premium paid to the club, of perhaps $10.00, when the put was sold, but that would leave their exposure at $20.00, still well above the current price of $6.13.

There are actions that could be taken to mitigate the situation, such as buying shares to dollar cost average in anticipation of the stock being put. The put could possibly be bought back and a new one sold.

The stock could be allowed to be put to the club, sold and then the club could sell a new put. The new put premium would keep things in profit and may also reduce the strike price involved. Alternatively, the traders could sell an additional put at a much lower strike price. Effectively, that would be using the sale of puts to dollar cost average. If the original put resulted in stock being put, the new put would have the effect of reducing the average price paid. The exposure would be further reduced by the additional premium income from the new put trade. If the stock isn't put on the additional trade, then the position will have improved because of the additional premium income it brought in. All the alternatives must be considered, and some simple calculations undertaken to allow an informed, logical decision on how best to take advantage of the price fall.

Sometimes additional put options are sold on a stock even when the stock is in overall profit. For example, one of the clubs owns 1,200 shares in BBBY. They paid $25.50 for them. They used the sale of puts to dollar cost average and have sold calls too. Their total income from the stock, before selling the new put, was $20.52 per share. Even with the current price at $6.13 they had a gain of $1.15. They decided to buy another 2,000 shares and negotiated a price of $6.00 for them. This brought the average price they had paid down to $13.31.

The club decided to sell a covered call on the newly purchased shares immediately after the shares were bought. The call had thirty days to expiry and gave a premium of $0.74 with a strike price of $7.00. If the shares were called away, the club will have added ($0.74 + $1.00) × 2,000 = $3,480, or 29% of the $6.00 share price they paid to the income generated on their original shareholding. That income would then be $23.42, which is almost 92% of the original purchase price.

If the club retain the shares, they will have reduced the average price paid and added $0.74 × 2,000 = $1,480 to the income column. Of course, in this event they will probably sell further covered call options in future months. Not bad for a stock that is currently under stress because of world events. There is nothing to stop the club going on to create more income from BBBY, even after they have more in income than the shares cost.

Accumulating free shares

The above was a real-life example of how a club is working its way towards owning shares that it doesn't pay for! This happens with many of the puts that the extraordinary investment clubs sell, when they result in share ownership. They sell puts at strike prices that offer premiums with an element of gain built into them and this provides free shares.

For example, Alkermes Plc (ALKS), a biotechnology company in the healthcare sector, has its shares trading at $27.01. The company has not suffered badly during the current pullback and its share price remains in an upward trend. The forecasts predict it could get as high as $50.00.

A $30.00 strike price put could be sold with an expiry date 154 days ahead, for a premium of $4.47. As the difference between the current price and the strike price is $2.99 and the exposure would be at $25.53, there is a gain of $4.47 − $2.99 = $1.48 built in. Across say 1,000 shares that is worth $1,480, which is enough to pay for forty-nine of the shares if they are put at $30.00. From day one of share ownership, there is the beginning of an accumulation of free shares without any dollar cost averaging or other actions.

Many of the techniques used by the extraordinary investment clubs provide free shares. The clubs quickly get to own shares of greater value than the members have invested, while retaining most of that investment to finance further trades. The effect is truly remarkable.

Risk-to-reward ratios

In addition to all the filtering undertaken to find trades involving sound companies at great share prices, the clubs also take notice of the risk-to-reward ratio inherent in each trade.

The BBBY stock, for example, at around $6.00 per share, has little scope for a big price drop, whereas it has the scope to rise to its forecast price of $18.00. The risk-to-reward ratio, in this case, is 1:3. The stock has scope to increase in price by three times its potential to fall.

The clubs don't normally take the potential for a stock price to fall as being all the way from its current price to nil. Instead, they find a significant low price point that has previously been visited, often several times. For many stocks, they are currently using the extreme low price that occurred in March/April 2020, when the Covid pandemic had its greatest impact on stock market prices.

The traders don't generally calculate the actual risk-to-reward ratio for each trade. A visual check and categorisation into high, medium or low levels of risk-to-reward suffices. Potentially high-risk trades are avoided; medium-term risk trades are carefully considered and they may make the trade smaller if it does go ahead.

Option drag and price drag

The terms 'option drag' and 'price drag' are used a lot in extraordinary investment club meetings and reports. Option drag is the amount of money due into a trading account in respect of unexpired put option premiums. Such premiums are paid immediately on the sale.

If the trade is modified, it usually involves an increase in the total premium. If a trade is closed early, the move has normally been planned to release buying power for another trade that represents a better opportunity or, if desired, just to increase buying power, if that is needed.

When members talk about the value of a trading account, they often include the value of option drag, but are careful to make it clear that this is the case. That is because some of the option drag may not come through if, for example, it is decided to close a trade early. Most of the premiums do come through.

Price drag occurs when a stock price is lower than that which was paid for it. Price drag is never included in any stock position or account valuation. The club members prefer to make shares profitable on price alone and to use option premiums as an additional income stream. Bear in mind that many of the shares owned were obtained for free!

Typically, share prices rise by around 50% above their average price and fall 50% below their average over the course of a year. That is yet another reason why the clubs don't get too excited by the highs and lows of prices for the stocks they own. They only get excited about the prices of stock that they don't own and about other gain-producing opportunities.

Return on investment and capital employed

Measures of return on investment (ROI) and return on capital employed (ROCE) are of vital importance to the clubs. The traders don't enter any trade without knowing what return they expect to gain from it.

Return on investment

When entering a new put trade, the extraordinary investment club members think of ROI as being the percentage that option income represents of the strike price. A put option premium of $5.50 against a strike price of $19.00 would represent a ROI of ($5.50/$19.00) × 100 = 28.95%.

These are basic calculations that are modified to consider commissions to be paid and money to be paid out for protective lid trades.

Return on capital employed

Increasingly, the clubs prefer to consider the ROCE as their main measure of performance. The 'capital' used in their calculations is the amount of SBP tied up by a trade. This is an excellent measure that allows the easy comparison and ranking of potential trades.

For example, the $5.50 premium on a $19.00 strike price put, as shown above, may use, say, $2,000 of SBP per 100 shares. The ROCE would then be (($5.50 × 100 shares)/$2,000) × 100) = ($550/$2,000) × 100 = 27.5%.

While 27.5% may sound good, it may or may not be acceptable to the traders, depending on how long the capital is tied up for. To get to an understanding of this, the return is annualised. If the 27.5% corresponds to 90 days, the annualised return would be (27.5%/90 days) × 365 days = 111%. If it was for a period of 350 days, the annualised return would be (27.5%/350 days) × 365 days = 28.68%.

The aim is to at least double the value of each club account every year. Therefore, the members are not normally interested in put trades with an annualised rate of return that is below 100%. The average annualised ROCE of trades currently on club shortlists is 187%.

Back in Part One, we started with a list of twenty-seven potential trades with an average annualised return of 141.5% and an average gain rate of $0.08 per day per share. Some of those eliminated from the exercise had higher daily gain rates than others that were retained. They were eliminated because of the amount of capital they tied up and the number of days they tied it up for. The excluded trades had annualised return rates of between 49% and 96%, which made them not good enough!

The potential trades are ranked and the traders work down the list, trading until the available capital has been used. Therefore, even trades with annualised return rates of over 100% are not always taken. If they got down the list and still had capital available, they would wait for better trades.

I should mention that in the first year or so of new funds being traded, the clubs don't expect to make a return of 100%. It takes at least six to twelve months to get to that sort of run rate. Even then, market conditions can slow progress.

Pullbacks and bear markets

In the middle of June 2022, the US stock markets – along with all other stock markets – were down, as measured by the performance of the S&P 500. It had peaked on 4 January 2022 and bottomed out on 17 June 2022 at around 24.5% down. Although starting from a higher base, the fall was of the same order as the fall at the onset of the Covid pandemic.

A fall of up to 20% is known as a pullback. Beyond that, we are in a bear market. Pullbacks and bear markets occur with a degree of regularity. At least one of them can be expected every two to three years, even in 'normal' times.

The fall brought a ripple of excitement among the members of the extraordinary investment clubs. They knew that:

1. The stocks they trade generally fall by a smaller percentage than the overall market.

2. Their stocks tend to recover more quickly.

3. The stocks in their portfolios tend to rise by more than the overall market as recovery comes.

4. Pullbacks and bear markets have always been less frequent and more short-lived than bull markets, which see stock prices rise relatively quickly.

5. They are well prepared for any pullbacks and bear markets by keeping a large proportion of their account value in cash and having many protective strategies in place.

6. Pullbacks and bear markets mean that there are lots of stocks to be had at bargain prices.

The club members worked out early on that it is scarier to be out of the market getting low interest rates than it is to be in the market. There are many stocks that double or even treble in price, but they first need to be owned and second need to be held with sufficient patience to take advantage of the rises when they come.

Volatility

In general, the club's welcome volatility in the stock market. When it is high, the premiums paid in respect of both covered call and put options are higher than when volatility is low.

Options are traded on the Chicago Board Options Exchange (Cboe), based in Chicago. The Cboe produces an index known as the VIX. This tracks overall market volatility and is inverse to the stock markets.

Therefore, when stock prices are low, the VIX is high and when stock prices are high, the VIX is low.

Like a stock, the VIX runs between support and resistance and tends to run in cycles of three rolls before changing direction. However, the support and resistance levels of the VIX are normally stable with support at a level around 15 and resistance at a level around 35. The VIX does, sometimes, move outside of these levels. At the height of the pandemic, it got as high as 85.

The clubs frequently use the VIX to time trades to get better option premiums if it is rising and to allow it to act as a warning to protect positions if it is falling.

Diversification

The members consider it prudent not to hold too large a proportion of their portfolios in any one stock or even in any one industrial sector. The target is to have no more than 5% of their investment in any one stock or sector. Industrial sectors can be hit by issues that are specific to them or to a group of sectors. For example, retail has recently suffered more than other sectors due to the economic woes of the war in Ukraine. Prior to that, we saw the car industry struggle to get the microchips it needed because of the pandemic.

This can prove difficult with smaller trading accounts. Their owners start the diversification process by aiming towards having 10% of their investment in each of ten companies across ten sectors. Bear in mind that they want batches of 100 shares in each company so this policy could represent 1,000 shares overall. However, shares come at different prices. We could have a mix that includes shares at, say, $5.00, $10.00 and $20.00 each.

With that mix and an account value of $30,000, having 10% in each would look like 600 of the $5.00 shares, 300 of the $10.00 shares and 200 of the $20.00 shares. Therefore, there is a need to adjust the number of batches of 100 shares being traded or to make other adjustments. They could step away from a share with a price of $60.00 as 100 shares in it would represent 20% of the account.

The next target would be to own stock in twenty companies with 5% of the value of the account in each. They would also want these stocks spread evenly, in value terms, across twenty industrial sectors or subsectors.

However, there are only eleven industrial sectors across the US stock markets:

- Energy
- Materials
- Industrials
- Consumer discretionary

- Consumer staples

- Healthcare

- Financials

- Information technology

- Communication services

- Utilities

- Real estate

Thankfully, the sectors are broad and they are broken down into subsectors known as industries. The subdivision used by Value Line includes ninety-six industries. Retail, known by Value Line as the consumer discretionary sector, includes eleven industries, or subsectors, such as apparel, automotive and hard lines such as furniture. Note there is also a consumer staples sector covering essentials such as food. The Value Line reports, and our assessment process, helps the clubs to find the best sectors and industries to trade. The clubs do need to be careful with their selections, as some of the industrial sectors are closely related.

Dividends

The extraordinary investment clubs don't often trade with the acquisition of dividends in mind. Dividends are simply that part of a company's profit paid out to shareholders in proportion to the number of shares they own. Not all companies pay dividends, and they represent a small proportion of the gains that the clubs and individual traders make.

As discussed earlier, when assessing a business the clubs want management teams to reinvest profits to grow their businesses. The resulting increase in share prices is of greater interest and benefit to the clubs.

Dividends can be paid out as cash or as additional shares. When a trading account is set up, these alternatives are usually given. Be sure to choose the cash alternative. If shares are taken, the number is normally quite small and the shares won't come in even batches of 100. As a result, when it comes to selling covered calls, there will be shares that can't be included in the trade. That means either just sitting on the 'spare' shares, selling them with commission representing a high percentage of the deal or buying more to round up and get back to batches of 100. Not a good idea if you like to acquire stock by getting paid to buy it through put sales. None of these are the most profitable choices.

TRADER PROFILE

Tom is a serving police officer. In recent years, like many in the public sector, he has had to accept some disappointing changes to his pension fund. The changes had a serious impact on his plans. He was looking forward to retirement and to then taking a less physical, less stressful job than frontline policing. The police pension would have allowed him to take a position with a lower salary.

It is not to be. The changes increased what he has to pay into the fund, reduced what he will get as a pension and require him to remain as a police officer for longer. Not only did the changes disrupt his retirement plans, but they also hurt his current standard of living by taking more of his income as pension contributions.

Tom cast about looking for another source of income to supplement his earnings and to try to bring his plans back into line with his wishes. The alternatives open to a serving police officer are few. He took on a part-time multilevel marketing business. Unfortunately, that wasn't as easy or as lucrative as it had seemed.

Then Tom found one of the extraordinary investment clubs. He hasn't been able to invest a lot, but has made sure he put something in every month. He has the major advantage of having time available for his investment to mature, with about ten years to go to his preferred police retirement age. That should easily be enough to replace – in fact to far exceed – his lost pension. If everything goes to plan, he won't need the lower-paid job after retirement and will be able to choose how he spends his time.

Summary

In this chapter I have tried to anticipate the questions that readers may have about how the clubs trade and to bring to their attention matters that they may not have considered. I have answered the questions that I would have asked if I was new to trading, knowing what I know now. I have also included what I think for most people are some of the unknown unknowns, as it was once famously put.

Much of the chapter has been concerned with getting out and staying out of trouble when it occurs, including trouble caused by market conditions and trader-caused issues such as overtrading. Defensive techniques were discussed covering both.

It should also be clear now that the extraordinary investment clubs look beyond the bare forecast increase in share price when selecting trades. They are also concerned with the ROCE and are constantly ranking prospective trades to find the best potential returns based on this.

Although I have covered everything I would want to know before getting involved in trading, I hope you stay with me for Part Three of the book. By the end, you may agree that a far easier route to making great returns would be to join a club and to learn among like-minded others than to work alone.

Part Two Summary

Nothing has been held back. I have explained exactly how the extraordinary investment clubs select and trade stocks. The reader could now go off, practise and become experienced at making money – albeit first on a simulator please!

In Part Two there was an examination of the strategies used by the clubs, including buy and hold, selling covered calls and selling puts. The results of selling covered calls and the six possible outcomes of selling puts were covered. It is because of these six outcomes that I can say that none of the clubs, across what is now more than 3,000 trades, have lost on any of them. Once more I have made a big claim! However, I am happy to stand by it and I am giving plenty of opportunity to all readers to verify it.

As well as the actual strategies used, there has also been a close examination of the most important of the many factors that need to be understood by traders beyond the basic strategies.

In the next part, I move on from trading to how the clubs operate as clubs. This was touched upon earlier, as and when necessary, as part of the explanation of trading. Now we will go into more depth.

PART THREE
MANY HANDS MAKE LIGHT WORK

You now have a good insight into how the extraordinary investment clubs identify and trade stocks on the US markets. You have, laid out above, all the knowledge you need to repeat their success. Yet, knowledge alone won't get you too far in most cases. Some of you may already be adept at trading and easily able to take significant steps forward after reading Parts One and Two. Most, though, will require more than just the information, needing experience and a safe environment in which to develop this knowledge into a skill.

For some, a trading simulator will be enough. After all, simulators allow everything to be tried and tested without fear of loss, over as long a period as anyone may want. Note, though, that everything changes from the moment people switch to risking real, hard-earned cash. It is like the difference between reading and knowing the Highway Code inside out and sitting behind the wheel of a vehicle on the open road, so take your time, start small and practise hard.

Not everyone is both willing and able to learn how to trade – especially from a book – or to learn the detail or become a proficient trader themselves. Some want to get to grips with trading in the company of others and to make money while they do it. Others may be happy to be relatively passive. I want as many people as possible to benefit from what we have developed, and for many that may be from within the extraordinary investment club environment.

In Part Three you will learn how the clubs work. The opportunity to come aboard as an observer will be given, as well as a chance to engage with members and ask them questions directly. At the time of writing, there are around 300 members. They are developing into a real community of like-minded people who are working together and successfully overcoming financial challenges, taking advantage of the financial opportunities that have been uncovered. Here is how that magic works.

SEVEN

How Extraordinary Investment Clubs Work

Investment clubs are covered by regulation and need to be properly constituted. That requires appointing officers, keeping records, treating all members equally and having high, democratic standards. There are many ways of achieving these things and these days technology, such as online meetings and video recordings, has transformed the opportunities to co-operate remotely.

The extraordinary investment clubs take the security of members' funds seriously. This is reflected in how they are organised. As far as possible, they separate banking and trading activity. Trust is hugely important. Thankfully, neither an extraordinary investment club nor any other member of the TICN network has had an issue with security – and TICN goes back more than twenty-five years.

Members can now be located anywhere, can access records directly, can catch up through meeting recordings and don't have to rely on minutes written by a club secretary. This is how they work.

Meetings

Frequency and duration

Much of the communication between members of the extraordinary investment clubs is through their dedicated WhatsApp groups. They use both WhatsApp and emails to remind members of meeting arrangements and to circulate links for them.

These days, the clubs invariably meet via Zoom. With an international roll of members, it is now the only practical arrangement. The extraordinary investment clubs meet at least once a month. The dates are given in advance and club meetings are usually held during the week in which the third Friday of the month occurs. That is because traded options expire on the third Friday and therefore there is a need for decision making on those trades that have expiring options.

When needed, additional meetings are called, usually with several days' notice. These are quite rare. An example of a reason for such a meeting could be that a club has a large amount of SBP and therefore a lot of trading decisions to be made.

Each club also has an annual general meeting (AGM). This is usually tagged onto a normal meeting and is used as a review of progress, to appoint or reappoint officers and to present accounts.

The clubs frequently have guests or observers present at their meetings. These could be people who are considering joining or members of other extraordinary investment clubs just dropping in to say hello. The meetings are open.

How meetings run

Apart from the AGM, meetings usually start with a review of what is happening in the overall market and a discussion of factors that may be influencing it now or in the near term. These are usually macroeconomic matters, such as wars, invasion, pandemics and similar. This discussion normally centres around the S&P 500 and sets the club's high-level view of how things are moving – whether it is going to be bullish or bearish, for example. Being bullish would lead to more trades, with higher strike prices and higher numbers of contracts. Being bearish would see the club holding back more, with fewer trades, lower strike prices and lower numbers of contracts per trade.

Next, the meeting reviews the latest monthly dashboard. This is a statistical record of stocks owned, prices paid, current values, cash flow, etc. They then go on to undertake actual trades. This involves analysing the forecasts and ranking possible trades. Many factors come into play. For example, does the club already hold positions that it wants to dollar cost average? Is it over- or under-exposed in any sectors?

If a lot of trades are to be undertaken, some may be executed after the meeting closes. Similarly, the club's traders keep an eye on things between meetings and may use their delegated authority to trade either when necessary or when good opportunities present themselves.

Recording decisions

Each extraordinary investment club meeting is video recorded. This not only provides a catch-up facility for those who couldn't attend, it also allows trading and other decisions to be recorded. Video recordings are not the only record of events. Detailed trading and ownership records are also kept.

Most meetings last just over one hour. They are recorded, edited and uploaded to YouTube as unlisted videos. The recording of the latest meeting is posted to the web page of the club involved, which also has the latest dashboard and future meeting dates on it.

These web pages are password protected for the privacy of the members.

Officers

Chair

The role of chair is more than that of a figurehead. The functions they undertake include:

- Being the legal 'agent' of the club. That means acting as the appointed representative of the club in dealings with the broker. All communications between the club and the broker go through the chair. All trades undertaken are confirmed and the confirmations are directed to the chair. As there is a cost and delay to receiving postal confirmations, these are usually received by email.

- Running the club in terms of chairing club meetings, ensuring that its business is conducted openly, properly and fairly, and that proper records are maintained.

- Enforcing the constitution and rules of the club. The chair is the final arbiter in any dispute resolution. Thankfully, this is not a function that most chairs ever need to undertake. Although I haven't ever seen it happen, in theory the chair has the job of being the final level of appeal if anyone is refused membership or if a person is asked to leave the club for any reason.

Treasurer

Being the treasurer involves being the main contact with the UK bank that each club uses to collect members' contributions and from which funds go to and come back from the trading account.

Frequently, the treasurer also takes on the role of keeping members abreast of how the club is progressing. The chair and treasurer need to be completely separate to allow security of members' funds to be seen to be a priority, as well as actually being important.

Traders

Traders can be a single person or, preferably, members of a trading committee. Their role is to recommend and execute trades. The trades can be executed within a meeting or, when necessary and appropriate, between meetings.

Each extraordinary investment club is supported by experienced traders who fulfil a coaching and mentorship role. In each case, the mentor is also a contributing member of the club, with a single vote like any other member.

The extraordinary investment clubs all belong to TICN, a support organisation with a ready supply of experienced, successful traders who are happy to coach and support them.

Attendance

Some investment clubs operate a strict attendance policy, under which failure to attend a minimum number of meetings each year can lead to expulsion. The extraordinary investment clubs don't operate such a policy. There is no doubt that better decisions are made with greater engagement and participation.

Members generally fall into one of three categories, though they can and do move between them over time. These are:

1. Regular, keen attenders who are fully engaged and get a lot from the meetings. A high proportion of these also have – or aspire to have – their own trading accounts.

2. Occasional attenders who probably attend fewer than half of the regular meetings.

3. Never/hardly ever attenders. Like all members they continue to be invited and get the reports on progress etc. They are members of the club's WhatsApp group and are on its email circulation list. They are always made to feel welcome if they do attend a meeting.

Some decisions, such as closing a club or taking a dividend, are exceptionally important. The members write into the constitution of their clubs a requirement for a minimum proportion of the membership to participate in making them. These decisions may be made at a club meeting, at the AGM, through a survey or through some combination of these.

Security

The extraordinary investment clubs are dealing with what most people consider to be large amounts of money. Trading pots of more than a million dollars are no longer considered exceptional. Therefore, members need to be confident and sure of the security of their funds, as well as knowing that trading is being properly looked after.

Openness

The first tenant of our security policy is to be as open as possible about everything to do with banking, the trading account and trading.

Bank account

The clubs keep as little money as possible in their UK bank accounts. There are per-transaction costs for transferring funds from the UK bank account to the US trading account. For this reason, they tend not to move small amounts. As soon as a UK bank account has accumulated around £2,000, a transfer is arranged.

Bringing funds back from the US trading account to the UK bank account requires the authorisation and signature of at least two members. The treasurer can't bring money back on their own authority.

The clubs have a strong, personal relationship with the bank staff and would immediately be notified of any proposed transactions that are large or unusual.

Trading account

Trading accounts are protected by usernames and passwords, which have a restricted circulation. In this regard, only the chair and traders have access to trade the account. The traders don't have the ability to transfer money out of the trading account back to the UK bank account.

Back office

Each club has a detailed back office account that is updated at the end of every trading day. All members have access to it.

The back office has a massive amount of information. For example, every trade ever undertaken and every movement of funds in or out of the trading account is listed there. All current balances are shown and any margin movements are also identified.

Documentation

Below are the main documents that members use to control their clubs and provide a basis for trading.

Constitution

Every club needs a constitution – a set of rules to operate by. There are significant advantages to having those rules written down and agreed in advance of a circumstance where they need to be referred to.

The constitution neither needs to be complicated or lengthy nor does it need to be written in legalese. It just needs to cover the basics:

- The name of the club

- Aims and objectives – simply the trading of stocks and options

- Members – minimum and maximum numbers, minimum age, acceptability of prospective members to existing members

- Termination of membership

- Level of investment required

- Appointment of chair, treasurer and traders

- AGM and other meetings, quorate requirement

- Rules and procedures, record keeping

- Finances – covering any costs, possibly a dividend policy

- What happens when members leave – or even die

- Time horizon

- Changes to the constitution

- Dissolution

The constitution needs to be signed by all the members, and the bank and broker being used will want sight of the document. In addition to signatures, the bank and/or trading platform will want full names with photographic proof of identity, including copies of passports or driving licences, addresses (and proof of addresses such as recent utility bills or bank statements), National Insurance numbers and a note of each member's occupation.

One of the trickiest elements of the constitution is recording the calculation of what is owed to a member who leaves or to the estate of a member who dies. It is tricky because leavers can only take away a share of the club that represents its NLV. At any time, most of the profits have been reinvested and a lot of the value is therefore uncrystallised. This can mean that the leaver gets less money than they paid in, even if the club is doing well. If positions must be closed early to facilitate paying the member out what they are owed, costs such as transaction fees and currency exchange costs could also need to be charged. The constitution needs to be specific about such matters so disputes are avoided.

Time horizon is included as a constitution element to deal with the matter of leavers not being able to take away uncrystallised profits. If this were not to be considered, there wouldn't be an opportunity for anyone to leave – ever, without losing a part of their share of the gains made!

The extraordinary investment clubs overcome the problem by having a five-year time horizon. In other words, they see the club being dissolved at the end of a specific, agreed-in-advance period. Then, as dissolution is approached, the trades being undertaken can be matched to the end date so there are little or no uncrystallised profits when the members are due to be paid what they are owed.

The clubs don't have to be dissolved for members to take money out. They can, by whatever voting requirement the constitution sets, take a dividend that will be paid to all members. The time horizon can also, if the constitution allows, be changed by the members. At the end of the time horizon, some or all of the members may choose to put some or all funds they receive into a new club to continue their involvement.

Form W-8BEN

Members need to determine their US tax status. In most cases, this involves completing a simple single-page form provided by the US government. This is known as Form W-8BEN. It is sent to the trading platform provider and refreshed every three years. US citizens will provide a W9 form.

Records

Accurate records are essential for two reasons:

1. It is just about impossible to keep track of positions without records. The trading platform provides a great record of current positions and a full history of trades undertaken. However, it doesn't show the cumulative effects of trades.

2. The members will want to know the overall position of the club and their own positions within it.

Trading record

It is through the trading record that clubs keep track of the cumulative effect of trades on the positions they hold. For example, a club sells a $20.00 strike price put and gets a premium of $4.00. The exposure is $16.00, even though $20.00 will potentially be paid for the stock. If the stock was put to the club and the club went on to sell a covered call against it, for a premium of, say, $1.00, the exposure would become $15.00. At this point, the trading platform wouldn't show the effect of the put premium or the call premium. It would show exposure as being the $20.00 paid for the stock. Because the stock was put to the club rather than just bought, depending on the broker used, the broker would need to be contacted to arrange for the trading platform to show the purchase price, be it $20.00 or $15.00.

Things get even more complicated when dollar cost averaging is used, particularly if there is a mix of stock at different prices, puts at different strike prices and with different expiry dates and some calls too.

A spreadsheet is used to keep track of trades and exposure levels. The spreadsheets show a lot of information about each trade. Forecast price levels, exposure, most-wanted rankings and SBP used being examples.

Dashboard

The dashboard is another spreadsheet. This one is produced at the end of each month to show the overall progress of the club. The information on the extraordinary investment club dashboards includes:

Total and average amount invested

The total amount invested is self-explanatory, but the average amount may need explaining. It is a reference to the average amount available to trade between the start of trading and the date of the report.

A total investment of $10,000 may have come into the club as $5,000 in month one and $5,000 in month twelve. On average, the club would have had $5,000 available to trade in that year. In this case, it would show the percentage increase in the value of the club against both the total investment of $10,000 and the average investment of $5,000.

Shares owned

The detail on this includes a listing of all shares owned, the number of each share owned, the price paid for them, their current value and their projected value in eighteen months and in three to five years. It also shows the industrial sector that the shares sit within. A pie chart displays the proportion of stock in each sector.

Option drag

In this section, the total value of unexpired put premiums is shown. The clubs see this as future income and liken it to a tradesperson undertaking work and then invoicing it for payment on a specific future date. Some of this income may not materialise if the club decides, for example, to close a put trade early, so they are careful about when to include option drag in club valuations.

These are the essentials, but the clubs often decide to include additional information, depending on what is happening in the account at the time.

Individual position statements

Club members want to know about the value of the clubs in terms of their personal position. This is achieved through the monthly publication of a separate spreadsheet that details the standing of each member.

The personal position spreadsheet starts with confirmation of funds that have gone into the trading account from each member in each month. This allows each member to know the proportion of the club that they own. It is also important to record when funds were contributed. This allows the value of the club to be distributed between members according to the contribution they have made to the average amount made available to trade.

The process is much like that of a unit trust. There is a points system with points determined by multiplying the amount of each contribution by the number of months that the contribution has been in the club. The points awarded collectively to all the members is used as a divisor to find the percentage of the club value, including the gain to be allocated to each member.

Back office

The dashboard and personal position spreadsheets are internal documents produced by club members.

It is important that members can also reference the finances of the club through independent, external sources. Those sources are the bank statements and the back office website of the clearing house that sits behind the trading account.

All members can access the back office directly at any time. Every movement of money, every trade and all balances within the trading account are available, and the data is updated at the end of every working day.

Using the above, each member can audit the internally produced dashboard and personal position spreadsheets.

Research

Earlier, we covered how the extraordinary investment clubs use data from the research company Value Line. The clubs also keep a close eye on business news from the USA. Some of the members even subscribe to *The Wall Street Journal*.

Members frequently contribute to the debate on which stocks to trade. For example, one club meeting recently included a detailed discussion on what was happening in the US airline and cruise line industries. The discussions can get quite lively and the feedback about them from members is positive.

Income versus capital growth

Any club setting up needs to decide on its aims and objectives. A main element of this is a decision about whether the club wants to produce a regular dividend-based income for its members or to work towards building as large a capital sum as possible, usually to be taken only when the time horizon date is reached.

Self-evidently, taking dividends on a regular basis has an impact on the growth of the capital base of the club. The clubs need to trade for around six to nine months to get into their stride in making gains. Almost all the trades involve expiration dates that are three or more months after the start date of the trade. It takes a further twelve to fifteen months to get to a position from which dividends can be taken without disrupting growth too seriously.

The dividends taken need to be small enough to allow some continuation of capital growth. If this is done, the size of the dividend can be allowed to increase, probably by more than the prevailing inflation rate over time.

Of course, club members can change the aims and objectives of their clubs at any time through a democratic vote. Nothing would stop a club, for example, concentrating on capital growth for several years and then moving to paying regular dividends. In these circumstances, the dividends would probably be higher than they otherwise would have been.

Tax

No one associated with the extraordinary investment clubs gives advice on tax matters or is qualified to do so. The clubs understand that Capital Gains Tax (CGT) is payable on positive differences between the price at which shares are acquired and the price at which they are sold.

Investment clubs are required to keep records, to let each member know when such gains are realised and to apportion them between the members in relation to the contributions they made to the trading pot.

Thereafter, it is up to individual members to let their tax authorities know about the gains. If the members are United Kingdom based, they may have a CGT allowance, which (at the time of writing) allows them to have gains of £12,300 per annum[8] before becoming liable to pay tax (if they are not already using their allowance for other capital gains such as those arising from property sales). Some members join with their partners or spouses to take advantage of having two CGT allowances.

---

8   GOV.UK, 'Capital Gains Tax: what you pay it on, rates and allowances', www.gov.uk/capital-gains-tax/allowances, accessed 14 October 2022.

Gains arising from the sale of covered call options and from put options may attract income tax, depending on individual tax circumstances.

Currency

As previously mentioned, the extraordinary investment clubs hold their trading accounts in the United States in US Dollars. In consequence, when funds are sent from or to the United Kingdom, currency exchange costs are incurred.

The trading account back office gives a full record of funds arriving in or leaving the account. That makes the task of keeping track of deposits, withdrawals and currency exchange costs straightforward.

TRADER PROFILE

Ron and Debbie work hard and have built a good lifestyle as a result. Things changed a short time ago with the unfortunate passing of Ron's father. His vulnerable mother couldn't manage on her own and circumstances meant that a care home was the best option for her. The couple were determined to ensure that she went into a care home that was a great place to be, with excellent care. They knew this was going to be expensive. Ron's mother's house was sold and provided a useful cash lump sum to help with the costs. The problem was that the money from the house sale would run out in too short a period.

Ron and Debbie were already members of an extraordinary investment club. They knew that the stock market could be a source of income that could pay the care home fees, while protecting and growing the capital that came in from the house sale. The club they were in had long-term capital growth as its objective and did not lend itself to taking money out on a regular basis to pay the care home fees.

Fortunately, when all these events were taking place, the Quarterly Income Club, a new club with income as its main objective, was just about to launch. The couple worked out what money they would need to pay the fees for a couple of years. Then they put the balance into the new club. They are confident that by the time they need the income to pay the fees it will be there. In what they see as the worst case, the capital sum will have grown significantly.

Summary

Investment clubs, by law, must be organised and democratic, and I can't think of any good reason why they wouldn't want to be either. In this chapter I have outlined how the extraordinary investment clubs fulfil these requirements.

Life is much easier if fair and reasonable operating rules are set out clearly, simply and in advance. Trying to determine what the rules of the game should be during a difference of opinion or dispute about a 'live' issue tends to end with the strongest personality and opinion winning out. Decisions made in advance of issues arising tend to have outcomes that are balanced and fair.

Sometimes investment clubs try to avoid appointing a chairperson. This is usually on the basis that all members are created equal. This is a mistake, as clubs need a final arbiter in the event of a dispute. Even member votes can have evenly divided outcomes. In practical terms, clubs also need a treasurer. The banks and trading platforms require named individuals as points of contact.

Similarly, an appointed trader (or traders) is essential. Chaos can result if more than one person is accessing and trading an account without coordination. Unfortunately, this means that the trading platform can't be made accessible to all members as individuals. I would like to see a platform that can be viewed by any member but can't be traded by everyone who accesses it. I haven't come across one yet. Remember, though, the back office and various spreadsheets can have shared access and the spreadsheets can have all member access, but with restrictions on who can alter them.

In practice, things soon seem to settle down. The clubs rarely resort to actual votes on any issue, refer to the constitution for guidance, to face removing members or to need decisions arbitrated on by the chair.

EIGHT

Support And
Learning To Trade

Continuous process development and learning are both features of the extraordinary investment clubs. Typically, tweaks and enhancements are made to research methods, trading and other processes every month. The clubs therefore have a strong ethos of ongoing training and development.

Every club meeting has a high training and education content. The clubs have found that training and educating all members – even those who are more passive – improves trading decisions and outcomes. The thinking put into decisions is better and the questions asked are more pertinent. The whole process works better.

Learning to trade

Basic training

The basic training course, accessible to all members, takes the form of a series of modules, each consisting of several video recordings. Some also have reference material. The training assumes no prior knowledge but is useful even to experienced traders looking for a more reliable trading methodology.

The course includes a detailed, practical explanation of how to open a simulated trading account. This allows learners to practise without risk. Using the learning to drive analogy, this is the equivalent of learning what the various controls, steering wheel, accelerator, etc, do and how they work. No one should consider a live account unless and until they can prove to themselves that they can trade successfully on a simulator.

The simulator closely reflects live trading, but using a fifteen-minute delayed pricing of stocks and options. One major difference is that if things get messed up, the simulator account can be reset or replaced with a fresh new one.

In meeting education

Each club meeting is a huge learning exercise. It starts by increasing the members' understanding of the overall market and what is occurring within it. Every month members learn from each other's thoughts about the market and what is happening.

The members go through each of the positions owned by the club and consider whether action is required to maintain any of them. They see this process repeated many times and become familiar and comfortable with it. Then they go through potential new trades and the members repeatedly experience the process of selection – again, it becomes familiar.

The dashboard and other club documents are discussed, giving members a good insight into how to measure performance. This greatly reduces the scope for misunderstanding or misinterpreting how the club is performing and frequently avoids a lot of angst.

The trading strategy of the club is also discussed. This educates members in terms of what options and alternatives are available and what the various benefits and potential issues are with each of them.

Advanced education

Members of the extraordinary investment clubs can take their education to a higher level by accessing an advanced online learning programme. This is much more detailed in comparison to the basic course. It is useful for all members and essential for those who aspire to become club traders or to trade their own live accounts.

The format of the advanced training is a series of short videos followed by questions, the answers to which attract scores. Once a minimum score is achieved, the course allows access to the next part of the material.

Live training

The extraordinary investment clubs organise at least two live education sessions in the United Kingdom each year. They normally choose a central location in the Midlands and run them over a weekend. The sessions are well attended and serve to build a strong community spirit among members. Live training isn't obligatory for club members and not everyone chooses to attend.

Usually, live training events start on a Friday afternoon with a review of progress and a revisit to the forecasting and stock selection processes in use. It is normal for refinements and enhancements to be introduced. This session also acts as a method of recalibrating how judgements are made. There is always a lively question and debate session, which gets rave reviews.

The Saturday sessions are usually all about option trading techniques and are a fantastic opportunity for the clubs and individuals to learn from each other. Even the longest serving, most frequent attenders universally agree that they leave this session with more knowledge, a deeper understanding and greater confidence. The trading methodology has many moving parts. It is much like reading a good book that enhances knowledge each time it is revisited.

On the Sunday, new, more advanced material is introduced. In this book you have had the curtain pulled back to reveal just a handful of the thirty-two trading strategies in the trading armoury of the clubs. As the trading ability and confidence of the clubs grows, they are introduced to more of the strategies.

Consider what the difference is between a good and a great footballer. When the ball lands at the feet of a great footballer, their knowledge, experience, physical ability and mindset provide them with a greater range of alternatives on what action to take. Before the ball lands, they have read the situation well and moved to the most advantageous location on the pitch. This mirrors the clubs' approach to trading and education. Thankfully, traders don't need outstanding physical capabilities. They don't need any of the advantages that an individual player or trader has. In the case of the clubs, the experience, knowledge and ability are within the group.

Webinars

Being members of TICN, club members can access free live weekly webinars. For example, each Sunday evening a Zoom webinar is held to review the charts of almost 200 stocks, identifying those that members may want to include in their watchlists. On Monday evenings, two individual stocks are reviewed in detail. On Wednesday evenings, another Zoom webinar goes through the stocks, examining the indicators used to identify those that match a range of parameters that may make them ready to trade.

Annual US visit

Pandemic travel restrictions allowing, TICN organises an annual visit to the USA. The primary purpose of this is to attend the AGM of Berkshire Hathaway, which is run by Warren Buffett and his partner Charlie Munger. The trip also includes visits to the NYSE, NASDAQ, the Cboe, Value Line, a research house and a brokerage house. The trip includes many training events and even an address by a trading celebrity.

Trading tools

Being members of TICN gives the extraordinary investment clubs access to a range of trading tools that are either provided directly by TICN or for which TICN uses the collective buying power of its members to reduce the cost of.

The tools include Value Line research and a list of stocks that have achieved the high scores on quality and value discussed earlier in this book. They also provide an invaluable worksheet, which clubs and members can use to easily evaluate the quality and

SUPPORT AND LEARNING TO TRADE

value scores of what are – according to Value Line –
the 1,700 highest-ranking stocks on the US markets.

The extraordinary investment clubs

There are currently six extraordinary investment
clubs. Each has different characteristics, but they share
a strong bond and a common trading philosophy and
draw on the same bank of trading techniques. A high
proportion of members join more than one club.

The portfolio of each club is unique. That is because
they started trading in different months in various
market conditions and introduced funds at different
rates. They also reach a range of conclusions in decision making and have varying approaches to risk.
Because of these factors, the portfolios are never mir-
ror images of one another.

The progress of the clubs needs to be seen within the
context of how the stock markets are currently performing. At the time of writing (August 2022) the
stock markets of the world had just had their worst
opening six months of a year since the 1970s. Between
the end of December 2021 and the middle of June 2022
the S&P 500 index fell by just over 24%. Many, if not
all, of the stocks owned by the clubs fell in price. Yet,
remarkably, all the clubs have defied market conditions to emerge from this bear market well ahead in
their gains.

The clubs have been able to take advantage of the low prices and have positioned themselves to profit greatly as the market recovers. By mid-August 2022, the markets had regained almost half of the ground lost in the bear market and all clubs were far ahead of where they were at the start of the fall. Below is a brief 'pen picture' of each of the clubs.

Fortune Investment Club

At the end of June 2022, the Fortune Investment Club members had sent $272,915 to their trading account over a period of fifteen months. They owned 16,396 shares in forty-one companies across thirty subsectors of industry. The shares were worth $256,334. In addition, they had $75,103 of unexpired option premium income and $30,324 of cash. The total value was $361,761. That was $88,846 or 32% more than they sent to the market. However, the average amount of money it has had available to trade was $156,875. The gain against this was 56.63% – even though the last six months of its fifteen-month history had been in a bear market.

According to Value Line, the three-to-five-year forecast value of the stock owned by the club was between their low estimate of $592,409 and their high estimate of $911,549. Taking the midpoint, the forecast is for the portfolio value to increase to $751,979. That would be an increase in the value of the shares alone of $495,645, or 193%. Of course, the club will be continuing to trade and grow. The shares owned will increase, option income will continue to be collected and dividends will be paid. The club has a reasonable expectation of seeing its value being more than $1.5 million by the time it reaches its sixty-month time horizon.

The Fortune Investment Club has mainly attracted members who want to put small monthly amounts, as low as £100, into their club. Some members have effectively paid money in advance, and that is taken account of when the gains are calculated. Similarly, not everyone joined the club at the same time and members joining after the start of trading have put money in to catch up with the investment and gains of the original members.

Fortune is still open to new members.

Diamond Investment Club

The Diamond Investment Club is similar in age to Fortune, having traded for sixteen months. It has attracted members with a little more disposable cash and, at the end of June 2022, it had sent $650,774 to the market. It owned 31,100 shares across more than thirty industry subsectors, worth $538,590; had $216,383 in cash; and had $252,857 of unexpired option income to collect. The total value of these assets was $1,007,830, putting the club ahead by 55%. The average amount of members' funds it has had available to trade has been $403,130 and the gain against this is $604,700, that is,

150%. The Diamond club has a reasonable expectation of being worth over $3 million when it reaches sixty months of trading.

The difference between the Fortune and Diamond Investment Clubs, apart from one extra month of trading, is the pattern and amount of members' funds going into them. The underlying performance is similar. As time progresses, the gains against the average funds invested will align.

The Diamond Investment Club is accepting new members.

The Sapphire Investment Club

Sapphire is one of our newer clubs. It has been trading for just nine months. Bear in mind that it takes the clubs six months to a year to build momentum. The Sapphire Investment Club members put $1,140,505 into the club through a mix of lump sums and regular contributions. It has accumulated 60,608 shares across about forty companies in more than thirty industrial subsectors worth $1,039,806. The club is fully invested with just $25,000 in cash and has unexpired option premiums of $266,366. The total value is therefore $1,331,172. That represents a gain of $190,667, that is 17% against the total investment and 30% against the average investment, which was $632,610. A reasonable expected value at sixty months of trading is around $4 million. This performance is similar to that of the Fortune and Diamond Investment Clubs when they had a similar number of months of trading.

While most of the clubs have members who belong to the same family, this is particularly the case with Sapphire. Spouses, siblings, sons, daughters – and in some cases all of the above – are members.

The Sapphire Investment Club is accepting new members.

The Quarterly Income (QI) Investment Club

The QI Club is different from the above clubs. Its objective is to trade for a year or so and to then produce, as its name suggests, a quarterly income for its members. All the members have come from other extraordinary investment clubs. They know how trading works and have had time to become familiar with the system and confident that it works for them. The members of this club have each contributed £100,000 to the trading pot, or are in the process of doing so.

The QI Club only started trading in May 2022. The collective total investment to date is $661,627. Already the club has 4,000 shares worth $38,316. It has $241,485 of unexpired option premiums to collect.

The savvy QI Club members bided their time and entered the market six months after the start of the bear market. This gives them an advantage over the other clubs that they are certain to use in full.

The first dividend should be around $10,000 to $15,000. The plan is to leave enough money in the club to keep growing the capital base. The growth means that the dividend level should be able to be increased by at least 10% per year. Meanwhile, the capital will also grow well in advance of inflation so that members can more than maintain the value of the cash they have invested.

The QI Club is accepting new members, but only from other extraordinary investment clubs.

The 100th Millionaire Investment Club

The 100th Millionaire Investment Club is a closed club, open only to members of an exclusive business networking group. Started six months ago, the club is performing well for the stage that it is at. Some of its members are also members of one or more of the other clubs mentioned here. They have used the experience from the early months of those clubs to get this one off to a flying start.

Tees Traders Investment Club

The Tees Traders Investment Club was the first that I set up. It has now operated for thirty-one months. The name comes from the River Tees, which I have always lived close to.

Tees is a special club. I consider it to be the home of the future. It is where I am teaching people not only how to trade but how they can support clubs themselves. The membership is strictly limited.

Each member of Tees has contributed £6,000 to the trading pot. Our objective – yes, I am a member of this and several of the other clubs – is to turn each £6,000 into over $1 million. We are working towards doubling each £6,000 ten times in around seven years. £6,000 is now $7,161. The progression we are looking for is:

$$\$7,161 \times 2 = \$14,322$$

$$\$14,322 \times 2 = \$28,644$$

$$\$28,644 \times 2 = \$57,288$$

$$\$57,288 \times 2 = \$114,576$$

$$\$114,576 \times 2 = \$229,152$$

$$\$229,152 \times 2 = \$458,304$$

$$\$458,304 \times 2 = \$916,608$$

$$\$916,608 \times 2 = \$1,833,216$$

Consider joining a club

I have tried to be as open as possible in writing this book, determined to explain exactly how the clubs trade. I want readers to have enough knowledge to allow them to learn how to trade successfully under their own steam. I realise that not everyone will want to trade by themselves and not everyone will be capable of doing so.

Incidentally, where I have seen people fail or need to ask for help has been when they didn't follow the systems that the clubs use. One of the biggest hurdles is boredom. Some people get bored when following what is a repetitive system. Another cause of problems is trading using old news for which the market has already adjusted.

Of the more than 300 members of the extraordinary investment clubs, many trade their own accounts, but not one has chosen to stop being a club member.

My aim is to bring the benefits of successful trading to as many people as possible. Most clubs have deliberately kept the minimum investment levels low to allow as much inclusivity as possible.

I invite all readers to find out more about how the clubs work and to talk to any or even all the existing members to confirm how the clubs perform and work.

TRADER PROFILE

Michael owns holiday rental property at one end of the United Kingdom and lives at the other! The properties have worked well for him, giving him both income and capital appreciation. He has always intended to sell the properties to supplement his finances at some point in his retirement.

Being a member of several extraordinary investment clubs, with substantial sums invested, Michael is now revisiting his investment plans. He has become confident enough to bring forward the date at which he can sell his property and retire from that sector. He has given himself more choice and less reliance on property.

Effectively, Michael has also better secured the finances of his family if anything should happen to him. They are not property investors, and he thinks managing the portfolio could be a burden to them. That isn't the case at all in respect of his club investments.

Michael's wife is also a member of the clubs. This is not only part of his tax planning – his wife is becoming familiar with the clubs and what they do. Therefore, if anything should happen to either of them, the other will be able to continue to take the benefits of club membership with knowledge of and confidence in what is happening.

Summary

I am obviously a great fan of the extraordinary investment clubs, but I am an even greater fan of the trading system that they use. In this book I wanted to explain how the clubs trade and to do it in such a way that anyone can learn to do it. To me, being a member of one of the clubs is the easiest way to learn and a way of using the methodology without having to become an expert in it.

I could have concentrated purely on the methodology, but to do so would have missed out the advantages that club membership brings to trading. It would also have meant that access to the benefits would have been restricted to only those who were willing and able to trade by themselves.

Part Three Summary

I decided to include, as Part Three, a full section on how the clubs operate as clubs. Hopefully, I have demonstrated that they are well run, democratic and open. Every member of the extraordinary investment clubs has access to online learning and is strongly encouraged to take up the opportunity to use it. Find out more at www.theextraordinary.club.

Not every member will be willing and able to become a competent trader. Some will be happy to have a basic understanding, while others aspire to become great traders. Every variation is accommodated in the training and education processes.

As mentioned earlier, the extraordinary invest-ment clubs use several communication technologies including Zoom meetings, webinars, video recordings and email. However, it is worth emphasising the use of WhatsApp. Each club has a WhatsApp group. They are used well and no one is inundated with too many messages. The groups aren't moderated so no chat about trades or trading is restricted in any way.

There is also scope for people to start their own clubs within the extraordinary investment club family. To get the full benefit of being part of that family, clubs probably need at least a dozen members. However, you may recall that the first extraordinary investment club started with just eight members and a determination to grow.

In summary, a little work and thought before an investment club sets out on its journey is a great investment with enduring returns.

Conclusion

Parts One and Two covered in detail how the extraordinary investment clubs select and trade stocks, telling you everything the clubs know that has allowed them to realistically target over 100% growth year on year in their capital. There is no doubt that they still have more to learn and master to further refine what they do. The process is one of continuous improvement. There are thirty or more trading techniques and strategies that they haven't yet even considered. These will, in due course, get the extraordinary investment club treatment. Who knows, they may yet have to lift their performance target even higher!

In Part Three, I described how the clubs operate, considering important matters such as security. It is now time to look at the overall objective – the reason for setting up and supporting the clubs, rather than just using the techniques described to make a lot of personal wealth.

A million millionaires

The extraordinary investment club project is part of something much larger. My partners Owen O'Malley and Ana Rodriguez, operators of TICN, have built and continue to build clubs in many countries. While I look after most of the UK and measure membership in hundreds of people, they look after the rest of the world and measure the number of clubs (rather than members) in hundreds. Together, our ambition, passion and dream is to bring the extraordinary investment club concept to enough people that we create at least a million millionaires.

The ambition is huge. We fully understand the scale of what we want to do. We also believe it to be achievable. We will happily support people who want to learn how to trade outside of a club environment, but working through clubs takes us closer to our target and is therefore our preferred operating mode.

We are also determined to prove that sayings such as 'you have to have money to make money' and 'if it looks too good to be true then it probably is' don't always apply. We have always been careful to ensure that membership of the clubs is affordable for as many people as possible.

Where appropriate, we absorb costs such as research and training fees to help people to get on board. We go into schools to deliver financial education. We welcome anyone and everyone who is honest into our world.

I am particularly keen to help people who are heading towards the end of their working lives. So many have had their finances ruined by recessions, the pandemic, redundancy, pension schemes and pension regulation changes, and they don't have enough time to start over and to build a decent retirement fund.

What we do can help the finances of almost anyone. Think of people with disabilities who frequently can't get decent employment or those caring for others; the list goes on and on. I want to open the minds of as many people as possible to the fact that they can make money from the stock market, starting with anything from not much to a large cash pile.

Next steps

Hopefully, you are now persuaded that there might just be a way that ordinary people, like you and I, can profit greatly from the stock market. Frankly, I don't expect anyone to start trading or to join one of the extraordinary investment clubs solely because of reading this book.

I hope I may have sparked enough interest in the minds of some people to prompt them to find out more about what the clubs do, how they work and how they perform. If, after appropriate due diligence, they would like to join us, they will most likely be welcome to do so. Let's not forget that the members have the final say on admission!

Ethical trading

As I wrote this book, a couple of thoughts occurred to me that didn't fit with any of the chapters about how to trade or how the clubs work, so I am covering them here.

Ethical trading

There are companies that some people have an ethical objection to trading the stocks of. Tobacco, some banks, the meat trade, genetically modified crops; the list could be long! We don't operate a 'banned' list within the extraordinary investment clubs. Instead, we rely on democratic decisions. If a member (or members) have ethical reservations about any company or sector, they are free to persuade fellow members of their case.

Giving back

The pursuit of money for the sake of having money doesn't do much for us as individuals or for mankind.

Club members are encouraged to give something back to society as their wealth grows. Giving to good causes is enriching for the giver as well as, hopefully, helpful for the recipients.

Trading the stock markets as we do within the extraordinary investment clubs is far from a full-time occupation. I estimate that a club member could spend as little as four hours per month on trading-related matters, even if they trade their own accounts. Eventually, this could facilitate people giving up their day jobs. If so, I hope they may consider giving back a little time to their community as well as or instead of giving money.

Another way of giving back is to introduce the extraordinary investment club concept to people you know who may benefit from it. Up to now, we have grown solely by word of mouth. I hope this book is going to make it easier for people to use word of mouth to spread the word. Just think, you could be part of our mission to make a million millionaires!

Final thoughts

The journey has been long within a relatively short book! At the start, it was explained why the extraordinary investment clubs concentrate on the stock markets of the USA, due to more available public information on company performance and the possibility of trading stock options in a profitable way.

The selection of stocks to trade was considered in some detail. The whole process of putting thousands of stocks into the selection funnel was gone through. It was noted that the clubs end up with around a dozen or so good-to-trade stocks each week through their analysis.

Then attention was turned to trading, where the magic happens. Trades and all their possible outcomes were examined. It was noted that all the outcomes can be profitable. Remember throwing a dice and knowing that it will land on a win, whichever side faces up when it lands?

Attention then turned to the clubs themselves and how they operate. Each club was described and looked at in terms of how they are doing at the end of the worst fall in stock prices in the first half of a year for fifty-two years. It was reported that they all came through with flying colours. Not only did they survive but they thrived, and are taking advantage of the bargain-priced stocks that became available.

Finally, I would like to invite you to come to one of the club meetings as an observer or to view a recording of the latest meeting of any one of the clubs that you choose. Also you are welcome to join the WhatsApp group of a club to see the chat and ask the members anything you wish.

You can also contact me directly with any questions at: jeff@myinvestmentclub.co.uk. I frequently have one-to-one Zoom meetings with prospective members and am happy to do so.

At this point, you now know about the extraordinary investment clubs, what they do and how they work. You have a route through which you can greatly improve your financial position, even to the point of reaching financial independence. That is not having to rely on anyone else to live what you consider to be a decent lifestyle or even to reach financial freedom, and having enough wealth that you never have to worry again about your finances.

The next move is yours! Knowledge without action is worthless, so open your mind, check us out and, if that goes well, get on board.

Acknowledgements

I have worked hard to develop techniques for identifying great trades and to work out how best to execute them. However, I have stood on the shoulders of a giant in the form of Owen O'Malley and now his life and business partner, Ana Rodriguez. I thank them both for the gifts they have given and their warm, enduring friendship.

Much is owed to my fellow members of the extraordinary investment clubs. Without them I would not have developed my knowledge and skills to the point they have reached. I may possibly have made a lot of money, but I would have missed out on so much more without them. So, a big thank you to them all.

I give particular thanks to those members who have agreed to appear in this book in the guise of trader profiles and to those who have read and helped with turning my first rough draft into a better book. In particular, I would like to thank Ana Rodriguez for her excellent technical proofreading and advice.

Finally, thanks to Benjamin Graham who taught investment to Warren Buffett, to Warren Buffett for all he has brought to the lexicon of knowledge of investment, and to Tony Robbins for what he taught Owen O'Malley.

The Author

Jeff Fitzpatrick had a successful corporate career and became a director of several blue-chip companies such as Magnet Kitchens and Silentnight. This culminated in his appointment as deputy chairman of manufacturing with GUS/Burberry, running sixteen factories making apparel, woven products and furniture.

He then entered the world of small business, employing twenty-seven people engaged in the support of small business start-ups. His company was involved in over 5,000 start-ups and made a significant dent in the statistics on early stage survival.

Jeff still owns a significant share in an engineering business that is working to replace conventional chipboard with an ecofriendly alternative. However, his main interest these days, apart from his family, is trading and supporting others in their journey to become successful traders.

He enjoys speaking and writing and is lively and entertaining in both. He is known for having a wicked sense of humour. Get in touch:

🌐 The Extraordinary Investment Club
The clubs

in Jeff Fitzpatrick

Printed in Great Britain
by Amazon

17992690R00123